THE BUSINESS OF DESIGN

PUBLISHED BY
PRINCETON ARCHITECTURAL PRESS
A MCEVOY GROUP COMPANY
202 WARREN STREET
HUDSON, NEW YORK 12534

VISIT OUR WEBSITE AT WWW.PAPRESS.COM.

EDITOR: LINDA LEE
DESIGNER: DEB WOOD

SPECIAL THANKS TO: BREE ANNE APPERLEY, SARA BADER,
NICOLA BEDNAREK BROWER, JANET BEHNING, MEGAN CAREY,
CARINA CHA, TOM CHO, PENNY (YUEN PIK) CHU,
RUSSELL FERNANDEZ, JAN HAUX, JOHN MYERS,
KATHARINE MYERS, MARGARET ROGALSKI, DAN SIMON,
ANDREW STEPANIAN, JENNIFER THOMPSON, PAUL WAGNER,
AND JOSEPH WESTON OF PRINCETON ARCHITECTURAL PRESS
—KEVIN C. LIPPERT, PUBLISHER

LIBRARY OF CONGRESS CATALOGING-IN-PUBLICATION DATA
GRANET, KEITH, 1956–
THE BUSINESS OF DESIGN : BALANCING CREATIVITY AND
PROFITABILITY / KEITH GRANET ; FOREWORD BY ART GENSLER.
— 1ST ED.
208 P. : ILL. (CHIEFLY COL.) ; 26 CM.
ISBN 978-1-61689-018-6 (HARDCOVER : ALK. PAPER)
1. DESIGN SERVICES. 2. SUCCESS IN BUSINESS. I. TITLE.
NK1173.G73 2011
745.2068—DC22
                                    2011000849

THE
BUSINESS
OF
Design

BALANCING CREATIVITY
AND PROFITABILITY

Keith Granet

Foreword by M. Arthur Gensler Jr.

PRINCETON ARCHITECTURAL PRESS, NEW YORK

THIS BOOK IS DEDICATED
TO MAKING DREAMS COME TRUE.

TO MY MOTHER, DOROTHY,
WHO TAUGHT ME HOW TO DREAM;

TO MY PARTNER, JON,
WHO MAKES MY DREAMS COME TRUE;

AND TO MY SONS, JOSH AND DREW,
WHO ARE MY DREAM.

CONTENTS

9 FOREWORD *M. Arthur Gensler Jr.*

13 INTRODUCTION

CHAPTER ONE
18 The Foundation of a Design Business

    Design Education 21

    Writing a Business Plan 24

    Starting Your Own Firm 30

    Strategic Plan 33

    Top Ten Business Practices 35

40 INTERVIEW WITH *Michael Graves*

CHAPTER TWO
42 Business and Financial Management

    Financial Tools 46

    Budgeting 61

    Contracts 66

    Managing Profitability 75

78 INTERVIEW WITH *John Merrill*

CHAPTER THREE
80 Marketing and Public Relations

    Marketing 82

    Building a Marketing Plan 87

    Public Outreach 88

    Finding a Niche 96

    Learning How to Say No 97

    Public Relations 98

106 INTERVIEW WITH *A. Eugene Kohn*

CHAPTER FOUR
108 Human Resources

    Finding the Right Fit 115

    Reviewing Your Staff 116

    Mentoring Your Staff 118

    Employee Benefits 124

    Hiring Practices 126

    Firm Structure 126

    Ownership Transition 129

    Building a Legacy Firm 132

    Corporate Retreats 133

138 INTERVIEW WITH *Victoria Hagan*

CHAPTER FIVE

140 Project Management

Project Kickoff 143

Team Structure and Roles 146

Scheduling 156

Budgeting 156

Contract Management 163

Technology and Project Management 166

Power of Communication 167

170 INTERVIEW WITH *Richard Meier*

201 CONCLUSION

202 ACKNOWLEDGMENTS

204 CLIENT LIST

206 INDEX

CHAPTER SIX

172 Product Development

Hiring a Licensing Agent 176

Product-Development Process 177

Negotiating the Deal 185

Managing the Deal 189

Licensing versus Self-Production 192

Building Your Brand 194

M. Arthur Gensler Jr.

Forty-five years ago, a college friend who was the development manager for a large commercial project was looking for someone to provide the tenant improvement and interior design for the building. I had never done tenant improvement—or even interiors—but being an architect, I thought, "I can do that." So I accepted the assignment, and I started on my way to opening my own firm.

Fortunately, my employer at the time let me work part-time in the mornings so I could focus on my new firm in the afternoons. In two months I was able to build some cash flow, gain an understanding of all the requirements of running my own company, and still have time to set up an actual business and a physical office. I really knew nothing about running an office, about business, or about interiors. But I had enough confidence to believe that I could take on this new assignment and still do a good job for my client. I certainly never realized that this small start-up would grow into the international design firm Gensler. I realize that the process would have been much easier had there been books and programs on how to run a business and develop a professional-service organization that I could have consulted.

The Business of Design by Keith Granet is a wonderful book that serves as an important resource for establishing and managing design firms. Keith provides many invaluable suggestions for designers and architects who want to start a practice or take their business to a new level. I have always thought that as a profession—since all ships rise in a rising tide—we would better serve our clients by running firms that are much more professional. Leveraging Keith's wisdom and expertise will go a long way in raising the bar for professional service firms.

I started my firm without benefit of a business plan or any formal business training. After a few years of practice, I realized I needed to take a course in business, so I enrolled in an extension program at the University of California. After three classes I knew that I wouldn't learn everything I needed to know quickly enough. So I hired my professor, Glen Strasburg, to work directly with the few key people I had brought into my firm. Glen led weekly classes and assigned homework to my team so that we were able to quickly learn what we needed about the business side of our efforts. I believe Glen eventually became the first business consultant to work with architecture and design firms, and it is especially exciting to see what Keith has done following Glen's example in both building his consulting practice and in providing support to so many firms.

When I look back at the beginning of Gensler, I realize that because we didn't have a strategic plan, we had to just chase opportunities, try to do the best we could on our projects, and then look again for new clients when the projects ended. I was very fortunate—although I didn't realize it at the time—that my first assignment connected me with a client with whom I worked for almost two and a half years. In addition, the people I met along the way introduced me to other clients, many of whom are still clients of the firm today.

Over the years I have learned one critical lesson: it's a lot easier to do great work and retain an existing client than to continually search for new clients. It can't be emphasized enough that in order to provide a great solution, an understanding of the client's needs and requirements is essential. No matter what area you are working in—residential, commercial, hospitality, etc.—you need to understand your client's needs. Each project is different, and each requires different skill sets, but the common thread that runs through all successful projects is understanding the client's needs.

Keith started as an intern at Gensler. He spent eight terrific years learning, exploring, and in many cases helping me and other people in the firm grow in their areas of expertise. When Keith left Gensler to start his own consulting business, it was obvious that he truly could add value to multiple design firms. I'm pleased that throughout the book Keith shares some of the skills he learned along the way at Gensler. It's equally important to note that not all of the recommendations that he makes were actually implemented. There isn't just one proven way to practice the profession of design. In fact, there are many successful approaches, but it's always important to have a plan, a goal, and to focus on achieving that vision.

I encourage others to follow some of the lessons I've learned over the course of my career. For example, I've never felt that I had to compromise my design approach in order to respond to a business requirement presented by a client. Actually, it's the other way around—understanding the business side will make you both a better designer and a better professional. It becomes a win-win situation.

I have a photograph on the wall of my office—of a Rolodex and a rubber band—that reminds me of two very important principles that I've learned over my career. My actual Rolodex cards contain all the names of the people I've met over the years and whom I've had the chance to both work with and learn from. The rubber band represents an approach that I've learned—not without some pain—over the years: it's better not to try to stretch a client too fast or too far. Architects have a tendency to want to put every creative idea they've ever had into each project. The fact that most Gensler clients are repeat clients is because we've stretched them—as with a rubber band—far enough to reach new levels but not so far that we've broken the relationship. If you stretch clients gradually, your relationship will have grown to the point where you've learned their needs and requirements by the time you've completed two or three projects together. You can then continue to do wonderful projects together and build your portfolio. The key is to treat those relationships with respect and honor. Listen to your clients and work with them. You'll soon build a better, more challenging, and more exciting practice.

As discussed in the "Human Resources" chapter of this book, another important element in building an organization is the quality of the people you hire. It's much easier to recruit people who are smarter than you and let them bring their talents to the organization than it is to provide all the ideas, all the leadership, and all the thinking by yourself. I feel the same way about consultants—whether mechanical, electrical, structural, or civil, or the firm's legal or accounting advisors. Hire the best and work with the best. I'd gotten to know some absolutely top people very early in my career, and I've stuck with them for the entire time of our practice. When you look for the best in your hiring practices, the return on investment will be far greater, and you'll have fewer problems along the way.

Whether you're an architect, interior architect, or designer, and whether you work for a large or small firm, or are on your own—you have chosen an excellent area in which to build a career. Being in the design field, you can have significant impact on your clients, your community, and the environment. Those of us in the business of design have the responsibility to provide sound solutions to the problems posed by our clients. What a wonderful challenge and tremendous opportunity on which to focus one's life's work. *The Business of Design* is a powerful learning tool that will help members of our profession, from new students to practicing professionals, understand these responsibilities.

INTRODUCTION

Designers and architects are some of the most creative people on earth. Their work is featured in glossy magazines; they dispense advice on reality TV shows. They've assumed celebrity status in our culture. But they can be some of the worst businesspeople I've ever met. They blindly trust their bookkeepers without having a system of checks and balances in place. They neglect to market their services during busy times, risking an endless boom-and-bust cycle. Many simply don't seem to care if they're properly paid for their services. We've all heard the joke about the architect who won the lottery. When asked how he was going to spend his new riches, he replied, "Keep practicing until the money's all gone." How can it be that people who are so talented, so committed, and so passionate about their work can sometimes be their own worst enemies?

That question is a big part of what inspired me to write this book. I've spent nearly thirty years helping design professionals achieve success. At Granet and Associates, I advise designers and architects on everything from billing to branding, from client management to marketing and licensing. I show them how confidence, discipline, organization, and good planning can help them run a business that allows them to pursue their passion for design and make a good living, too. I helped one firm grow from eight people to seventy. I advised another firm to shrink itself strategically so that it wasn't taking on work just to meet its payroll. I've helped many clients double or triple their incomes by charging for the value, rather than by the hour. And I've worked with clients to identify the disruptive personalities in their offices in order to make staffing changes that resulted in greater efficiency and healthier morale—and a better bottom line.

I provide my clients with the tools they need to make informed decisions about whether to take on a new job or client, hire an employee, or assume additional expenses that are in line with a firm's long-term goals. I was once told by a client that he sometimes wished that he could hand a potential client a check for $5,000 just to "go away," because he knew that if he took on the project, he'd probably end up losing ten times that amount. Many designers and architects see any new project as a solution to cash-flow problems, even if the designer-client fit is a poor one, and the project drags on to the point that it becomes a money loser rather than a moneymaker. I help clients see the difference.

Another common misconception is that only superstar designers command the highest fees and the best licensing deals, when in fact, there are people out there who are hardly household names yet have done very well financially because they know how to run a successful business. That kind of success involves not just the day-to-day workings of a design practice. It also requires the ability to recognize both opportunities for growth and the preconceptions that might stand in the way of that growth. That's why many of my clients refer to me as their "office shrink." I want this book to offer everyone in the design world, not just my clients, the tools to create a thriving design business.

My passion for design was evident in my childhood by the large size of my Lego collection. I was lucky to have parents who indulged my passion. I invested hours in designing and building Lego villages. As an undergraduate studying art and architecture, I spent a semester as an unpaid intern at the San Francisco office of Gensler and Associates/Architects (now called Gensler). After three months of crawling through buildings to create as-built drawings, rubbing letters off on vellum, and looking at talented architects with master's degrees who made $18,000 a year, I thought, this is not for me.

When I returned to school, I enrolled in some business classes and did very well. I thought that if I could combine my innate business sense with my love of design, this might direct me toward a career path. It was my "aha!" moment: I realized that I could put this talent to work while staying connected to the design world that I loved.

I tell you this story for one reason: it's my belief that for people to be successful, they must be passionate about the work they do. I had tremendous enthusiasm for the design profession, but I also knew that my real passion lay in the business of design, rather than in design itself. If either of those components had been missing, I would have failed. Success in design comes to those who have a little bit of both, business sense and creative talent, or at least the good sense to collaborate with someone who can complement their strengths and weaknesses.

The truth is that any profession is not solely about the skills it requires, but also about all the components it takes to build a successful career in that profession. You need people to market, manage, and run your company. Depending on the company's size, one person might need to have all these talents, but more often, they're divided among many.

For those whose real passion is designing, it's important to remember that design is a business, too. Teaching a designer to think about his or her business as a business first is not an easy task. Most designers love their profession more than just about anything and see it as such a labor of love that they'd even do it without getting paid, if they could afford to. This starving-artist syndrome is a major reason why so many designers are paid so little. I have many successful clients who make a lot of money in this profession, and it's because they understand the *value* of their work and how to charge for it. Some of them have an instinctive sense of their worth, while others need some coaching. But I'd say that very few designers and architects are taught to value their work. Nor are they taught much else about how to earn a living.

In fact, after all these years in the design profession, I realize that it's not just the creative mind that struggles with the profession's business side but also the education of that mind that does not serve its students well in the real world. There's a common misconception that students don't need to know the business of design. "They'll have a lifetime to figure out the real world. This is their time to live in a fantasy world and just design," one of my clients once said to me. But do students really enjoy not knowing, and not learning the business, until after they graduate from school? I don't think so. We teach our students to isolate their designs and present them to others only when required or to be critiqued. This doesn't encourage interaction in the design process, but in reality design is all about collaboration. Working in a vacuum, like they teach you in school, is not the answer.

So how do you learn the business of design? You learn it by working for successful practices, and you learn it by trial and error. This book is intended to help you learn it without having to make too many mistakes first.

Whether you're a recent graduate or a seasoned professional, this book will help you navigate the business of running a design practice. My suggestion for the young graduate is to go work for someone else and be a sponge, soaking up all the knowledge you can about the profession before heading out on your own. On the other hand, you may never want to open your own business—working in a larger firm gives you greater access to different types of projects without having to manage the business functions. My advice to the seasoned professional who reads this book is to put your habits aside and be open to new ideas for running your business. For the student who is taking a business class in design school and reading this book, as long as you have a passion for this profession, you'll be able to learn all the skills described here.

One day while on vacation, I thought about what it takes to succeed in any profession. I thought of all the successful people who had crossed my path, and the common attributes that they shared. I came up with six ingredients that I believe create true success:

1 **COMMON SENSE:** the world is too hard to navigate without it.

2 **GOOD KNOWLEDGE:** a thorough understanding of your business, but not necessarily to the point of overeducating yourself. The world is full of overeducated derelicts.

3 **CHUTZPAH:** the ability to take risks

4 **TALENT:** you need to find your particular talent.

5 **DISCIPLINE:** the ability to work at your passion a little bit every day

6 **PASSION:** the love for something that defies explanation

After each chapter I've included interviews with designers and architects who've made their mark on the profession, to share the benefit of their experience as well as their take on the business of design. I've also included experiences and lessons from my own life. I want to do more than write a how-to book; I want to improve the profession I love.

The first chapter explores the options you have once you graduate from design school. Vision and mission statements from other professions as well as the design profession are discussed. The chapter gives you an outline for writing a business plan and includes my top ten business practice tips for any design professional.

Chapter 2 explains the profession's financial systems that include billing and fee structures for budgeting both officewide and project-specific budgets. The chapter goes in depth to explain the importance of the financial tools available to a design firm to help run the company more effectively.

Chapter 3 explains the significance of marketing and public relations and offers insight into what they mean to a design firm. Marketing can be used to attract new work, new employees, and new relationships, and can be particularly useful in the new era of social media and internet connections.

Chapter 4 discusses the role of human resources in a design company. In a professional services industry, nothing is more important than how you treat your employees and how you mentor and motivate them to do their best work. This chapter addresses everything from hiring and firing techniques to delegating and mentoring methodologies and creating a rewarding and nurturing environment for you and your staff.

Chapter 5 takes you through the steps of project management and the need to communicate with all stakeholders to allow for a smooth and successful experience. This chapter focuses on the need for transparency with your employees to allow them to manage their projects effectively. The tools illustrated in this chapter were created for both internal and external players in a project.

The last chapter explores the trend in the design profession to develop products. Product development continues to grow as manufacturers recognize the need to bring expertise to their product lines. This is not a new concept, but it has become increasingly prevalent in recent years.

I hope that what you're about to read will guide you through a territory that many designers feel is uncharted. I wrote this book partly to share the lessons I've learned, in hopes of helping you avoid the mistakes I've seen other professionals make. This book is meant to give you the tools to create a bright future in a magnificent profession that has the potential to create beauty every day.

CHAPTER 1

The Foundation of a Design Practice

The business of design is a topic that baffles many, yet it's less tricky than you might think. Designers love what they do and will do anything to practice their craft. The key word here is *craft*. It's an art to design beautiful things, but it's a skill to execute these things of beauty in a successful and meaningful way, and still find room for profitability. The bottom line is not what designers worry about first. Look at these words: client, contract, negotiate, retainer, staff, design, draw, shop, expedite, present, budget, invoice, payment.

How many of them actually involve design? Only a few truly deal with the design process. The rest refer to the business aspects of design, so why is it that schools focus on the smaller fraction of the practice and at best offer one or two classes dedicated to the larger one?

The design profession has been around for thousands of years, and in the beginning, architects and designers were held in high regard. They served kings and queens, and were treated with the utmost respect for their craft. But somewhere along the way, the profession transformed from a title of distinction into one of subservience. (There are, of course, exceptions to this statement, evidenced by the designers who have achieved celebrity status due to their entrée into product design or television.) While many clients respect design professionals, many more believe that designers and architects are simply the hired help. You hire a lawyer because you need legal advice, and you see a doctor because you want to be healthy, but you don't absolutely need a design professional to build or design your project. Hiring a designer is considered a luxury. Yet as a luxury profession it doesn't command the respect of the business world in the way other professions do.

The real estate profession consistently receives a 6 percent fee every time a building is sold. An architect often struggles to get that same fee for creating that building and will receive it only once during the life of the building. This is because real estate professionals banded together to create a standard that the public finds acceptable. When architects tried to establish a similar standard through the American Institute of Architects, they were accused of price-fixing. In the decorating world, if you ask ten designers what their fee structures are, you'll get ten different answers. This variability confuses the general consumer of these services: if there's no established scale for pricing, you can't trust that you're being treated fairly.

Years ago I went to a big-box electronics store to buy a new telephone. I noticed that a competitor had a much better price for the same phone, and when I told the salesman that I'd seen the same phone for fifty dollars less, he offered me that price. Suddenly, I didn't trust that any price in the store was real. It put me in the position of establishing the product's value. If we in the design profession allow our clients to negotiate fees, will they really believe that the services are actually worth the price quoted in the first place?

The profession of architecture is a business, and technical knowledge, management skills, and an understanding of business are as important as design. An architectural commission might involve preparing feasibility reports, building audits, the design of a building or of several buildings, structures, and the spaces within them. The architect participates in developing the client's requirements for the building. Throughout the project (from planning to occupancy), the architect coordinates a design team and structural, electrical, mechanical, and other consultants. Even though this is the generally accepted definition of the profession, architectural education does not address it. It teaches only the art of design, not the art of the business.

DESIGN EDUCATION

Let's take a look at design education. If you want to be an architect, the schooling looks something like this: either you enroll in an accredited five-year program and receive a bachelor's of architecture degree, or you can continue for an additional year and receive a master's of architecture. You can also follow the more traditional route of a four-year liberal arts degree followed by two or three years of graduate school toward a master's of architecture. In the interior design field, you can pursue a four-year bachelor's of interior design degree, or you can simply call yourself an interior designer, since this profession currently has no educational or licensing requirements. A lawyer with an advanced degree can take the bar exam and become licensed to practice law. But a degree in architecture does not automatically make you eligible for the exams you need to pass to be licensed. In fact, you can't even call yourself an architect until you're licensed, and you can't become licensed until you've completed 5,600 hours or two and a half years of training under a licensed architect, before you're even eligible to take the licensing exams. This is why fewer than 25 percent of architectural-school graduates have a license to practice architecture. It's also surprising to learn that in 2009, a first-year legal intern could earn up to $70,000 a year, while a first-year architectural graduate would earn up to $45,000 a year—with almost the same length of education.

You have a real passion for design, and you know you don't want to be a lawyer. You stand there with diploma in hand (or not, in the case of some interior designers). What do you do next? There are basically two choices if you want to practice your craft: You can join a firm and start your work life surrounded by people who have knowledge to share. In this case, hand this book over to your new boss. Or you can start your own design firm (but you can't call yourself an architect or sign your own drawings unless you're licensed). If you choose this route, make sure you hang on to this book for dear life.

If you join a firm, be a sponge. Take in all that you can about every aspect of the practice. Learn everything you can about the projects you're working on: the vision behind a project's design, the terms of the contract, the design process, the project's construction. Understand who all the players on the team are, internally and externally. Observe how the people around you interact with each other and how they navigate the design process, the business process, and the people process. Being alert is the key to your growth and future in this profession. If you choose to work for a firm, the diagrams to the right show the traditional paths you can expect to follow. FIGURES 1 AND 2

If you choose to go from school directly into your own practice, which I don't recommend, then you should be prepared for years of trial and error in getting your business right. Minimally, a couple of years of learning from others will prove invaluable. I also highly recommend participating in an internship while you're still in school.

When you're ready to open your own firm or partner with another individual, you should have several tools in place. First,

ARCHITECTURE FIRM HIERARCHICAL DIAGRAM

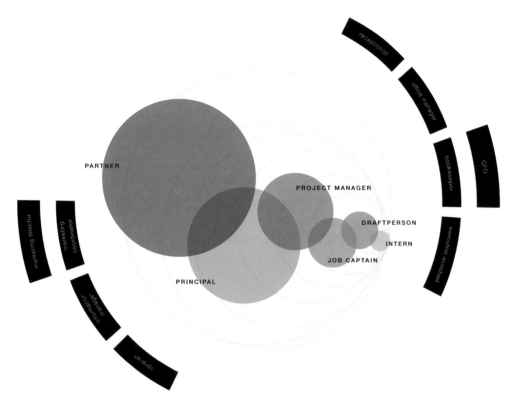

FIGURE 1

This graph demonstrates the path of the architect and the supporting staff needed for a thriving architectural business. The circles are the technical evolution of an architect from first joining a firm until he or she reaches the position of partner. The bars that surround the chart are the positions of support that are needed to run a healthy, vibrant architectural practice. They are also layered, in the case of CFO/bookkeeper and marketing director/coordinator. In both cases the bar closest to the circles represents the first layer of need for these categories and as you grow the second layer on need then comes into play.

INTERIOR DESIGN FIRM HIERARCHICAL DIAGRAM

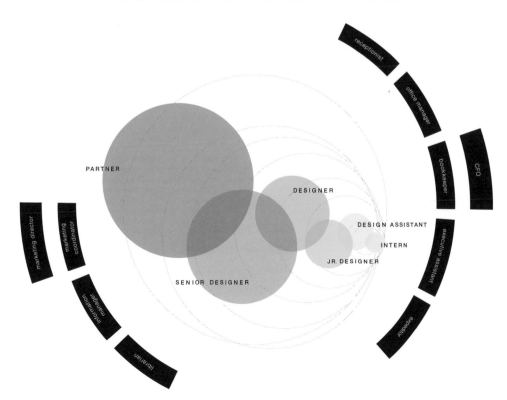

FIGURE 2

This graph demonstrates the path of the interior designer and the supporting staff needed for a thriving interior design business. The circles are the technical evolution of an interior designer from first joining a firm until he or she reaches the position of partner. The bars that surround the chart are the positions of support that are needed to run a healthy, vibrant interior design practice. They are also layered, in the case of CFO/bookkeeper and marketing director/coordinator. In both cases the bar closest to the circles represents the first layer of need for these categories and as you grow the second layer on need then comes into play.

you'll need a business plan. Some people believe that a business plan is a magical tool to achieve their goals. It isn't, but it can be used as a road map to reach those goals. FIGURE 3

WRITING A BUSINESS PLAN

When starting to write your business plan, you'll want to begin with three key elements: a vision statement, mission statement, and your firm's core values. A vision statement is the highest level of purpose for your business. The vision is a lofty goal that most likely will take your entire career to achieve. Someone once told me that having a vision is like the stars: we're better off for having them in our lives, but we may never reach them.

SAMPLE VISION STATEMENTS OF NONDESIGN COMPANIES:

"To make people happy" —DISNEY

"To preserve and improve human life" —MERCK

"To be the most respected brand in the world" —AMERICAN EXPRESS

SAMPLE VISION STATEMENTS OF DESIGN COMPANIES:

"Lake|Flato believes that architecture should respond to its particular place, enhance a site or neighborhood, and be a natural partner with the environment." —LAKE|FLATO

"Design can elevate the human spirit." —KAA DESIGN

"Redefining what's possible through the power of design" —GENSLER

"To create environments of an alternate reality, with compelling emotional force" —JOHN SALADINO

"The ultimate house of luxury now and forever" —CHANEL

A mission statement is used to help you achieve your goals. It sets the direction for you to reach your vision, for example, "Our firm should be a place of growing and learning for all our employees." This means that to achieve your vision you'll need to support, nurture, and mentor your staff. Another example might be that you want "an inspired environment to work in," and this

CONTENTS OF A BUSINESS PLAN

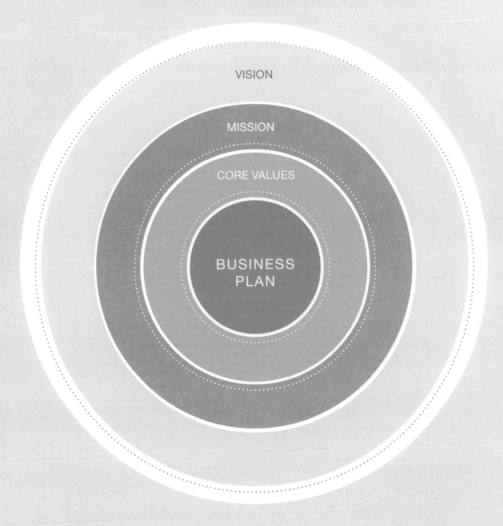

VISION

MISSION

CORE VALUES

BUSINESS
PLAN

FIGURE 3
Business plan content
hierarchy

may require a well-designed workplace, a healthy environment that allows people to be inspired, and an open environment in which to learn from each other.

SAMPLE MISSION STATEMENTS OF NONDESIGN COMPANIES:

"SOCIAL: To operate the Company in a way that actively recognizes the central role that business plays in society by initiating innovative ways to improve the quality of life locally, nationally and internationally. PRODUCT: To make, distribute and sell the finest quality all natural ice cream and euphoric concoctions with a continued commitment to incorporating wholesome, natural ingredients and promoting business practices that respect the Earth and the Environment. ECONOMIC: To operate the Company on a sustainable financial basis of profitable growth, increasing value for our stakeholders and expanding opportunities for development and career growth for our employees." —BEN AND JERRY'S

"Everything we do is inspired by our enduring mission: To Refresh the World…in body, mind, and spirit…to Inspire Moments of Optimism…through our brands and our actions. To Create Value and Make a Difference…everywhere we engage." —COCA-COLA

"eBay's mission is to provide a global trading platform where practically anyone can trade practically anything." —EBAY

SAMPLE VISION STATEMENTS OF DESIGN COMPANIES:

"The central concern of the practice is design excellence. KPF is committed to providing designs that create uplifting spaces for people. Our architecture responds to community, context and environment. Our work demonstrates the contribution architecture can make to sustainable patterns of living." —KOHN PEDERSEN FOX

"In lieu of subscribing to fashion and polemic, Richard Meier & Partners aims to deliver thoughtful, original and contemporary architecture that conveys a sense of humanism and purpose while fulfilling programmatic requirements. This is achieved through an intensive collaboration with clients and consultants and careful investigation into the best ways to accommodate the program. Richard Meier & Partners exercises economy of gesture and scrupulous attention which results in the highest standards of execution, delight in pure beauty, and respect for the client's need to be inspired and engaged."
—RICHARD MEIER & PARTNERS

"Rottet Studio is founded on the idea of providing innovative architectural solutions characterized by precise detail and direct response to the client's goals. Reflecting a desire to improve the human experience through the built environment, clients receive intelligent design admired for enhanced functionality, efficiency, flexibility and productivity, without sacrificing design integrity."
—ROTTET STUDIO

Core values are the guiding elements of your belief system. No matter the circumstances in your business or your life, you never alter these values. They're at the heart of what drives every decision you make in your career.

SAMPLE CORE VALUES:
> Education
>
> Excellence
>
> Fun
>
> Integrity
>
> Listening
>
> Quality
>
> Respect

You'll notice that making money and profitability aren't on this list. They're the by-product of all the work you produce and of the way you go about producing the work. I always tell my clients that if you are true to your values and create your best work, the money will follow. Sample core values specific to design (you might find these core values more applicable to a design firm, but there's no reason that all the previous ones wouldn't be appropriate as well):

Community

Context

Design

Livability

Sustainability

A TYPICAL BUSINESS PLAN ALSO INCLUDES THE FOLLOWING ELEMENTS:
1. Strategies, goals, tactics
2. Critical strengths
3. Finances (goals/budgeting, cash management, investments)
4. Products
5. Customers
6. Marketing (publication controls, brochures, website)
7. Competition
8. Market size/Locations
9. Management/Personnel (office structure, recruitment, employee benefits, growth opportunities)
10. Operations (project management, technology)

All of these areas are discussed in the chapters to come.

Once you have a vision statement, mission statement, and core values in place, how do you go about starting to practice? FIGURE 4

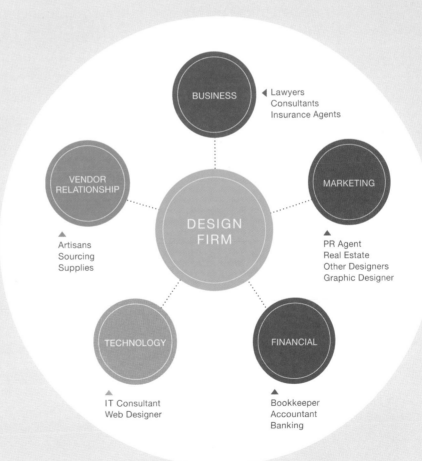

FIGURE 4
A sampling of design firm logos

FIGURE 5
Design firms that partner with outside resources tend to thrive more than the ones that try to do it all themselves

STARTING YOUR OWN FIRM

It's important to determine whether you'll be able to afford an office to start your business or whether you need to start out of your home. Many of the great designers started out of their garages and moved into offices once the work was flowing and they needed to hire more people. In my case, I needed to get out of my house to avoid the refrigerator and the television. Finding office space was more about my sanity and less about the need for a different space. I found that once I had a small office, I could focus on my work. I also had a place to hire my first employee and a place for clients to visit me for meetings that they didn't want to have in their own offices.

In the beginning, so much depends on how much money you have to set up your new practice. If you have the capital, I recommend getting a small space outside your home. You'll also need to think about the other costs associated with opening an office, including equipment (computers, telephones, printers, copiers), brand identity, website development, printed marketing materials, design software, accounting software, furnishings, and resource materials (books and catalogs).

The next steps to consider are relationships: financial, marketing, business, technology, and vendor. FIGURE 5

❶ FINANCIAL

You'll need to set up checking and savings accounts, and lines of credit.

→ **Bookkeeper:** To produce your monthly financial statements and reconcile your bank statements, invoice your clients, collect funds, and pay bills.

→ **Accountant:** To file your taxes and review your financial statements.

❷ MARKETING (SEE ALSO CHAPTER 3)

→ **Graphic designer:** To create a logo and design your stationery and promotional material.

→ **Public relations agent:** To help spread the word about who you are as a company and to make sure that you're not the "best kept secret."

→ **Real estate agents/developers:** These can be sources for new work, and developing strong relationships with them can help bring in new clients.

→ **Design consultants:** A resource as needed. They can also lead to project referrals.

→ **Interior designer/architect:** Depending on your practice, to share work or collaborate on projects where your skill set is needed.

→ **General contractors:** They can be a tremendous source for business, and having a solid relationship with a couple of contractors builds a resource for future work.

3 BUSINESS

→ **Lawyer:** To review design contracts, office leases, equipment leases.

→ **Management consultant:** To help create fee structures and negotiate your contracts, and to assist in developing your business plan and strategic plans.

→ **Insurance agent:** To make certain you're well protected in all your insurance needs.

4 TECHNOLOGY

→ **IT support:** Someone to understand your IT needs and to help with computer problems and software and hardware solutions.

5 VENDOR

→ **Alignments:** Establish relationships with vendors with whom you'll work regularly, for example, office supply vendors, printers, company credit accounts. Especially in interior design, finding great sources for products and services is what will set you apart from other designers. It'll also distinguish you to have access to great artisans who can bring added value to your projects.

With your business plan in place, office space figured out, standard contract in hand, and many of your business relationships established, all you need is your first client. I guess you could say you're dressed for the dance, you just need to find the ballroom. Or as one of my first clients once said to me, "We're like a fine-tuned race car looking for the track." What we learned was that sometimes it's easy to get so preoccupied with locating the track that you don't realize the *car* was the problem. There are many kinks that may need to be worked out initially, but it's imperative to recognize the importance of having the foundations of the business in place so that you can focus on the work.

The design profession, like many others, is as much about who you know as it is about how you design. In other words, you may be the most talented person on the planet, but if no one but you knows that, then your chances of working on great projects will be limited. You need to get out in the world and meet people and find the work.

Your practice will be far more successful if you can rely on repeat business coming from referrals rather than always seeking new clients. The relationships you build with your clients, your community, and your peers will bring you work. If you make yourself visible, people will remember you and what you do. This will allow them to consider you for their next project.

There was a time in the late 1980s and also recently (2002 through mid-2008) when you could simply say you were a designer and there'd be work for you. From 2002 to 2008, firms were turning down work left and right because they had more than they could handle, and the only thing stopping them from growing was the lack of available talent in the marketplace. New graduates were naming their salaries. Notre Dame University had more firms show up at its job fair than it had students to be hired. Then came the fall of 2008, and the faucet was turned off. Firms saw projects shutting down daily, and current clients became terrified to spend a single dime on a design project. Early spring 2009 brought more hope and a sense of calm that allowed people to assess their net worth and know what they could and could not do. Eventually the projects came back, though slowly. What became strange for most people was that they were coming off their best year ever to a year of little or no new work. Layoffs became a daily occurrence, and management consultants were asked for survival plans instead of strategic plans.

The real lesson to be learned here is to run your design practice as a business, and you'll be prepared for whatever comes your way. Plenty of firms struggled in the good times because they never focused on running a business, and the bad times weeded out the firms that weren't stable or nimble enough to manage through the downturn. In a design practice, the operations are the background noise, and the systems discussed in this book quiet that noise and allow you to do your best work.

STRATEGIC PLAN

Some people talk about their business plan, and some talk about their strategic plan; I'm often asked the difference. A business plan is a road map for setting up and running your business, while a strategic plan allows you to take one or more strategies within your business and formulate a plan to achieve a desired result. Typically, people develop their business plan before determining or creating a strategy. For instance, if I ran an architecture firm that worked with many landscape designers, and I decided to set up a landscape department within my company, I'd write a strategic plan for achieving that goal. Its contents might be similar to a business plan, but they'd be more specific to a single strategy or multiple strategies.

If you decide to add a discipline to your practice, like a landscape division, the process might look like the following. First, identify the strategy, then create a vision for the strategy and determine what your goals are for the strategy. Once you've defined the goals, break down each goal with a tactic that eventually gets the desired result. Other considerations include defining what additional needs you have outside your core business: deciding whether to buy a practice or hire and train professionals who have the desired skill sets; determining how to run the marketing; setting financial budgeting and goals for the new division; fulfilling staffing and resource needs to develop the strategy; and creating a timeline to achieve the strategy.

Think of it as running a marathon. You don't just decide to sign up and run a marathon. You determine that it's your goal to run, and then you start training, a little bit each day, to get your body prepared for the big run.

ASK YOURSELF THE FOLLOWING QUESTIONS:

1. Who will run the division?
2. Do I need a team now or can that wait?
3. How do I get work?
4. How do I build a portfolio to continue to get work?
5. How will I market this new division?
6. Do we need new stationery, a logo?
7. What kind of capital do I need to start this endeavor?
8. Do I have adequate space if I need to hire new staff?
9. Do we need to create a new/combined contract to service the work?
10. Are there any specific technology needs (software/hardware) to run this department?

The reason for a strategic plan is to help you make the right decisions, and to determine why you desire to shift your firm's focus to a new strategy and the implications of that shift. When companies that Granet and Associates has worked with jump into an idea without thinking it through, they tend to fail with their strategy.

In later chapters I talk in depth about all of the facets to the art of running a successful design firm. Plenty of illustrated design books on the market can inspire your design, but few books exist to guide you through creating a business foundation for your firm that gives you greater space to focus on design.

TOP TEN BUSINESS PRACTICES

To end this chapter, I offer you my top ten business practices, which are elaborated in much greater detail throughout this book.

❶ EVERY FRIDAY ASK YOUR BOOKKEEPER to give you the following: bank balances, list of checks received that week, accounts receivable statement (who owes you), and accounts payable statement (who you owe).

❷ HAVE THE CHECKING ACCOUNT STATEMENT come to you unopened. There is plenty of fraud in design firms, where there are significant dollars running through the firm and the financial person is tempted to think that a couple of thousand—or, in some cases, millions—of dollars won't be missed. The easiest thing to do is to write a check and then, when the statement comes, to destroy the check, and no one will be the wiser. These people always get caught, but it's a painful process and one that's almost brought down some design firms.

❸ REVIEW YOUR FINANCIAL STATEMENTS monthly and analyze them quarterly. You'll always be on top of your company's financial health this way, and you can also address any trends quickly and make corrections to avert a major financial crisis down the line. FIGURES 6 AND 7

❹ LEARN HOW TO SAY NO. This may be the best lesson you'll learn from this book. We all know when our gut tells us that a client or a project is not right for us, but we don't always listen to our gut when we need work or are enticed by a charming or famous client. Saying no to the wrong client and to the wrong project is what will save your sanity, save your reputation, and ultimately save your firm. You should learn as much as you can about potential clients and their history in working with designers. And just listen to your gut—it'll serve you well every time. (Look for my next book, *How to Be a Good Client.*)

❺ THE 10 PERCENT FINANCIAL RULE. I explain this in detail in chapter 2, so I'll just say here that the rule suggests that you take 10 percent of your fees out of your project budgets to allow

EXECUTIVE SUMMARY - ARCHITECTURAL MONTH ENDING 9/30

CATEGORY	CURRENT PERIOD SEPTEMBER	CURRENT PERIOD BUDGET	YEAR-TO-DATE	YTD BUDGET	PRIOR PERIOD AUGUST	PREVIOUS YEAR
INCOME AND EXPENSE DATA						
Total income	$435,039	$450,000	$3,800,602	$4,050,000	$402,900	$375,455
Reimb. Inc. Less expenses	$11,008	$12,000	$92,567	$108,000	$8,434	$9,008
Project Related expenses	$82,045	$75,000	$698,003	$675,000	$78,004	$85,109
Overhead Expenses	$156,003	$145,000	$1,345,603	$1,305,000	$198,007	$126,217
Net Profit	$78,307	$100,000	$702,004	$900,000	$81,203	$89,004
Overhead %	1.68	1.53	1.60	1.53	2.13	1.37
Break-Even	2.68	2.53	2.60	2.53	3.13	2.37
LABOR RELATED DATA						
Total Net Fees	$332,994	$335,000	$2,800,504	$3,015,000	$320,980	$297,348
Direct Labor	$93,004	$95,000	$840,009	$855,000	$93,004	$92,089
Indirect Labor	$25,012	$22,000	$201,903	$198,000	$26,503	$19,230
Effective Multiplier	3.58	3.53	3.33	3.53	3.45	3.23
Staff Utilization	75.00%	78.00%	74.00%	78.00%	77.00%	72.00%
Other Financial Data						
Cash on Hand - Checking	$285,023				$305,987	$191,004
Cash on Hand - Savings	$356,009				$345,804	$234,980
Line of Credit Outstanding	$0				$25,000	$45,000
Accounts Receivable	$957,086				$1,022,304	$1,203,380
Accounts Payable	$21,304				$28,450	$35,657

FIGURE 6
This is a dashboard to review your company's financial performance on a single piece of paper. See the text that follows for a more detailed explanation of each line.

KEY FINANCIAL INDICATOR GRAPH

	MAR	APR	MAY	JUNE	JULY	AUG	SEPT	OCT	NOV	DEC	JAN	FEB
Gross Income	532697	627558	518700	525000	549000	498000	505000	515000	602000	625000	548000	598000
Net Income	432000	498000	398000	405000	435000	415000	425000	435000	515000	520000	457000	500000
Direct Labor	165000	172000	149000	155000	170000	135000	155000	156000	169000	170000	158000	167000
Overhead	200000	212000	212000	203000	210000	215000	220000	221000	198000	250000	225000	298000
Profit	5000	100000	0	25000	45000	2000	5000	8000	120000	80000	60000	30000
B-NI	515000	515000	515000	515000	515000	515000	515000	515000	515000	515000	515000	515000
B-GI	425000	425000	425000	425000	425000	425000	425000	425000	425000	425000	425000	425000
B-DL	160000	160000	160000	160000	160000	160000	160000	160000	160000	160000	160000	160000
B-OV	216000	216000	216000	216000	216000	216000	216000	216000	216000	216000	216000	216000
B-P	49000	49000	49000	49000	49000	49000	49000	49000	49000	49000	49000	49000

FIGURE 7

Key financial data that aids you in seeing trends in your company's financial performance for a contingency and potential efficiency in managing a smaller dollar amount. People manage the money they have access to, and this way you'll have a contingency available that won't eat into your profits. In addition, I also recommend that with every check you receive, you take 10 percent of the funds and put them in a savings account. You'll be surprised by the amount of money that can accumulate after a short time.

6 COMMUNICATE. Share as much information as you're comfortable sharing. In fact, you should get comfortable sharing almost everything with your core staff. We work in a profession that, for some reason, doesn't share, and there's paranoia about sharing financial information with employees. The more information they have, the more they can do with it. But don't just share the data, share the purpose behind the data. Numbers are just data. How you formulate these data is called information; how you use that information is called knowledge; but how you assess that knowledge is called wisdom. Make people wise, and they'll make you more successful.

7 REVIEW YOUR STAFF REGULARLY. I address this in chapter 4, but there's nothing more important to your employees' growth than reviewing them and setting goals for the year ahead. It's also important to understand that reviews are not for disciplinary actions. You need to address issues as they occur and not hold them until a review. This not only will be ineffective but also will eat away at you until the issue is addressed.

8 ALWAYS PROMOTE FROM WITHIN FIRST. If you don't have the talent you need in your firm, then you have to look outside for it, but in the end you'll always be far more successful if you grow your staff from inside your organization.

9 LOOK FOR WORK WHEN YOU'RE BUSIEST. This is often difficult, because you tend to be focused on the work you already have, but if you wait until you need the work, it's too late. You should always be looking for work; there's a true skill in knowing when to take on the work and how to make clients wait for you until you can handle new projects.

⑩ SAY GOOD MORNING AND GOOD NIGHT to your staff. I know this seems trite and doesn't look as if it belongs in a top ten business practices list, but trust me, it does. If people are working hard for you, you need to acknowledge it and make them want to work harder. A simple good night and, better yet, a thank-you when you leave in the evening will work wonders. I went to a prep school whose motto was "Where manners count as much as math." I know, there were lots of issues with teaching that to an eighth grader, but it was a lesson that I've carried with me my entire life, and it's served me well.

> "I find that the harder I work, the more luck I seem to have."
> —*THOMAS JEFFERSON*

Michael Graves

KEITH GRANET: Who inspired you when you were thinking about being an architect and building your practice?

MICHAEL GRAVES: A lot of people. It wasn't by choice; it just happened that way because I went to the University of Cincinnati as an undergraduate, which is a cooperative school: we worked for two months and went to school for two months, worked for two months, went to school for two months.

By the time I got to Harvard, I had more experience than anybody else. I did work for a very short time for Walter Gropius, but in Rome. I worked for George Nelson in New York. George was very generous with me, and he liked me. There were fifteen or twenty people in the office; it was a real family. I still have some of those friends today. George was a furniture designer and a graphic artist as well as an architect. He never personally marketed his things the way we have.

Then you had an architect like Philip Johnson, who had done nothing but support younger architects all his life. He was just one of those people who wanted to know what the younger generation was thinking about. If somebody came to him with a commission he might lose money on himself, he would recommend a younger architect. Not so someone else would lose money, but because a younger architect might have a business structure that would allow him to work for less, and also so that he could earn the experience and perhaps learn something about doing another building type. There are architects who have done nothing but criticize other architects, and there are architects like Philip Johnson, who have done nothing but support them.

KG: Early on in building your practice, did you find doing competitions was a necessity to give you the expertise to get more projects of the same type?

MG: Early on I was asked to do a lot of back porches and kitchen renovations. What it led to was more kitchen renovations until my students called me the "cubist kitchen king," and that just kept the doors open in the sixties. But I was still losing money.

You have got to do a lot of these small projects. You have to be very efficient. You have to bang them out. I didn't do that. I spent far too much time on them. But they got published, and ultimately I got something else from these little pieces, because they would win awards. But it took a long, long time and a lot of money to do that. I suppose you don't start out being a brain surgeon when you're twenty-five. We submitted to a competition to design a stadium for the Texas Rangers baseball team, knowing that we didn't have much hope of getting the commission but that it would help establish credibility for going after other major stadiums.

KG: Do you consider the Portland project a turning point?

MG: Certainly. But the only reason it was a turning point is because we won. It was not a competition but a three-stage interview process in Fargo, North Dakota, for an art center that consisted of a museum, galleries, and a concert hall. I did a scheme for that, but it didn't get built, because a golf course was built instead. The art center was so heavily published everywhere that I got a lot of lectures at various places. I went to speak, I think to the AIA in Portland, and afterward the person who was the professional adviser for the competition said, "What would we have to do to get somebody like you to enter the Fargo competition?" I said, "Ask." But it meant that we had to put a team together of builder/contractor/developer, along with the architect.

KG: So the art center was a design-build project?
MG: Yes. Part of that was my skill in—I will take a little credit here—putting together a group of people I knew I could work with, and not trying to do this whole building myself. I hadn't built any city halls at that point in time or large-scale office buildings. So I collaborated with a firm that had built more office buildings than anybody else in the world, the firm of Emery Roth. We did prevail, but we got flack from the local architects for doing a building that wasn't "modern," as they wanted it to be.

After the Portland building, I was included on a number of competitions: there was one in San Juan Capistrano, California, that we won, and the Humana building (Louisville, Kentucky, 1982), which we won. We hadn't lost a competition at that point. We've lost a lot since then, but we were clearly on a roll. Having to win competitions to build buildings was not the best thing in the world for me; I mean, it kept me poor, because we were expending more money to make a better mousetrap each time.

KG: Do you think that the general public thinks that competitions are sort of a healthy way to find an architect?
MG: I think it's kind of a view of architecture as a commodity, something to pick and choose, like a pair of socks. I like a blue one. I like a green one. I like a brown one. I suppose people think it's more equitable. Many people don't have the experience of working with architects, and they don't know how to do it.

I meet people all the time, at various gatherings, who say, "Well, we wanted the kind of building you would do, but we knew we couldn't afford you. So we went with Joe Smith, our neighbor, and asked him to look at your work and do something like that." They never took the time to call up and ask what we charge. They really don't know.

KG: How would you identify the ideal client?
MG: Clients have to be—to a certain degree—savvy. I have one very good client, a developer of shopping centers, whom I met on the board of the Whitney Museum. He is a client who pays attention. He looks very carefully. He is not somebody who would come to you after the building is built and say, "Oh my God, I didn't know that you were proposing those kinds of doors." He is present, and he cares about details, dimensions, and the character. Not just about money, timing, or design, but all of the facets that he—or we could say ideal clients—should care about.

KG: Last question. How would you like to be remembered?
MG: I don't think about that very much. My mother once said that the important thing is to put more in than you take out. That's about it—make a contribution.

CHAPTER 2

Business and Financial Management

Business and financial management don't need to be a foreign language to designers. The finances of your business are your lifeline; without solid financial systems and an understanding of what it truly takes to run your business, you'll be distracted by what I call "the background noise of your business" in chapter 1. You know these noises: they're the sounds of worry that keep you up at night, the voices that you hear in your head asking where that next project is coming from or how you'll pay the rent or make payroll. These noises never really go away if you're responsible for the firm's livelihood. But you can lower them so that they no longer keep you up at night.

If you put the systems in place that are outlined in this chapter, you'll have the tools to keep informed about financial- and business-related issues. And you won't have to read thousands of pages of financial data. A good bookkeeper or controller and certainly a chief financial officer can create these documents for you in a way that's less of a burden to understand and gives you peace of mind. For years I've been presenting financial data to my clients in an easy-to-understand, graphically compelling way that, in fact, they look forward to seeing each month. As the key stakeholder, or for that matter anyone who's even the smallest stakeholder, you're responsible for understanding your company's financial health. Time and again, firms have hired me because the principal couldn't understand why the company wasn't making any money when everybody was working so hard.

A couple of years ago I was hired by the owners of a prominent interior design firm to help restructure their practice after they learned that their bookkeeper had embezzled $3 million. Now, this isn't General Motors; this is a small, successful interior designer. You can imagine my first question: how could you not miss $3 million? The answer was that it happened over a fairly long period of time. The bookkeeper took small amounts each month from the design firm client's profits on the sale of furniture—even though the firm was marking up the furniture at 35 percent, it was only making 25 percent profit. It wasn't until the bookkeeper actually got greedy (as embezzlers always do) and started taking more that the firm's accountant starting looking into the problem. The point here is that ultimately it's your responsibility to oversee your company's financial controls.

When I tell my new clients how important it is for them to put these systems in place and to be responsible for their firm's finances, I get a very typical response: "I'm a designer and I need to trust the people I hire to handle the business side, otherwise I'll be taken away from my job as a designer." Nothing could be farther from the truth. Remember those background noises. They exist because you don't trust the people in those positions, and you don't trust the tools you have to keep you from worrying. If you have these controls in place, they'll free you up to design more, and you'll do better work because of them.

Sometimes it's not only about looking at the numbers. In this profession many designers are guilty of loving their work so much that getting paid for it simply is not a priority. One of my first clients, a prominent residential architect, came to me because he said he'd been in practice for twenty years, but the business was nowhere near as lucrative as the perception the client had of his business. He asked me to examine his books and figure out if there were a way to make more money. The firm was known for its high level of service and high level of client hand-holding.

What I discovered in reviewing the books and the project financial reports was that he wasn't following the language in his own contracts that allowed him to increase his fees should construction costs increase. When you base your fees on the cost of construction, you're entitled to raise your fees as those costs grow. This protects you if the project expands in scope—your fees will also increase to compensate you for the true size of the project you're designing. In this case he was not increasing his fees, which left tens of thousands of dollars on the table, simply because he didn't want to nickel-and-dime his client. It wasn't that costs went up because the client kept picking more sophisticated materials: the client had increased the project's scope and detail, causing a significant change in the construction costs, which were the basis for the architect's fee.

Unfortunately, he was the typical architect who thought that as long as salaries and overhead were paid for, he was doing well. The truth is, his reputation allowed him to charge almost whatever he wanted, and clients would pay for it because the work was *that* beautiful. Today, after almost sixteen years of consulting with Granet and Associates, this architect finally has a lucrative business. In fact, he was able to build his own home and now lives like his clients. I share this story with you to demonstrate that at the end of the day, this is a service business that also happens to produce beautiful things. If you have talent, your time should be worth a lot. If it takes you ten minutes to design a detail, is it worth only ten minutes of your time? It's taken you a lifetime to figure out that detail, and it should be worth more than the time you spent in drawing it.

Value is a misunderstood word, but most people understand it when they truly feel it. When you spend a lot of money for clothes and they fit perfectly, or when you stay at an expensive hotel and the service is impeccable, you understand the value. The same goes for design: if clients understand what they're agreeing to in their contracts and you give them the best service and you don't surprise them ever with an invoice that they're not expecting, they'll pay their bills and pay them on time.

Once you appreciate the value you bring to the table, it'll be easier for a client to perceive that value. It's difficult to identify your own value no matter what profession you work in, but once you figure it out and deliver it, getting paid for it is much easier.

But to demand your highest fees, you need to have good business systems in place. Whether you're opening a new practice or you have an existing one, these systems are necessary for running your business. Let's start with the financial tools.

FINANCIAL TOOLS

You should have a fully integrated accounting system that can handle all functions of your firm. In architecture I recommend the software called Deltek Vision; in interior design, Studio Designer. These two programs consistently provide the most comprehensive data to run a design practice. Examples of the reports generated by these systems are found throughout this chapter. The features of a fully integrated system include the ability to create monthly financial reports. Most of these reports should be able to be run on two methods of accounting: cash and accrual. The cash basis reporting shows the dollars received (income) and the dollars spent (expenses) in the month. The accrual method shows the dollars billed (income) and the expenses booked, but not necessarily paid, in the month. The accrual method is a much more accurate way to look at your company's financial health; the cash method is used much more for tax reporting. These reports include income statement, profit planning report, balance sheet, general ledger, cash journal, accounts receivable report, accounts payable report, project-related reports, project progress report, project summary report, time analysis report, purchasing reports, summary reports—all at a moment's notice with the push of a button.

INCOME STATEMENT

This is also called a profit-and-loss statement and can be printed in a cash or accrual version, depending on the information you're looking for. Most of the time, accrual reports are used to examine a company's monthly performance. They compare monthly income and expenses resulting in a profit or a loss for the current month as well as the year-to-date information for your firm. This is an important tool to export certain key financial data and determine how you're performing within the industry you work in and to assist you in understanding any problems that may exist in either the billing or the expense side of your company.

PROFIT PLANNING REPORT

Depending on the type of system you're working with, this tool has different names: an *operational budget report* or an *actual versus budget analysis*. The purpose of this tool is to compare every line item on your income statement with each item's budgeted amount. This report can be compared both from an accrual and from a cash basis method of accounting. Some items may be fixed costs, such as rent; others, like marketing expenses and any unexpected expenditures that you've chosen to invest in during the year, will vary from month to month. You should make your best effort to create an annual budget to determine if you're on target with income and expenses and if they're aligned with what you intend to earn or spend. This is one of my favorite tools for clients, because they truly know where every dollar is being spent and what every one of their own clients is being billed. If the report shows a loss, it's an important tool to figure out how to correct or manage the problem; if there's a profit, to learn how to continue to do things right. One thing to remember about this information is that it's at least a month old. By the time you see it, there isn't much you can do, but you can correct the situation by understanding the source of the problem. It's also important to use other reports that help you monitor your company's weekly and daily performance. FIGURE 1

BALANCE SHEET

This report can also be shown as either cash or accrual, depending on your needs.* A balance sheet has three sections. The first is a list of all your assets: cash, accounts receivable, investments, equipment, and any other asset the company may own. The second is your liabilities: the items you owe to others, loans, accounts payable, retainers on account from your clients, and any other debt, such as credit lines and credit cards. The third lists the equity that tells you what your business is worth on paper: it's simply the difference between the company's assets and its liabilities. If your equity is high, it means that your assets outweigh your liabilities; if your equity is in the negative, you're losing money, and the company isn't making enough money to carry the debt it currently carries.

The balance sheet is something that you'll want to look at monthly to follow your cash balances and your accounts receivable and accounts payable.

GENERAL LEDGER

This report tracks every entry that's posted against your financial statements. This detail is vitally important when reviewing your financial reports, because it allows you to review every entry to see if an amount seems out of line for the month. The general ledger also details exactly what expenses are posted to a certain account. For example, if the office supplies account seems unusually high, the general ledger will indicate the actual charges that have been posted against that account. Your supplies may have just been restocked, or you may find that an error was made in entering the expense,

*For a sample report, visit www.thebusiness ofdesign.net.

Profit Planning Monitor

Apple & Bartlett, PC

As of period 6/30/2010

		Current	Budgeted Current	Bdg. Variance Current	Budget % Current	Year-to-Date	Budgeted YTD	Bdg. Variance Year-to-Date	Budget % YTD
	Revenue								
401.00	Billed Labor Revenue	140,137.10	345,833.00	(205,695.90)	-59.48%	4,176,577.65	4,149,996.00	26,581.65	.64%
402.00	Unbilled Revenue	18,185.00	(65,035.00)	83,220.00	-127.96%	(799,425.00)	(780,420.00)	(19,005.00)	2.44%
	Subtotal	158,322.10	**280,798.00**	**(122,475.90)**	**-43.62%**	3,377,152.65	**3,369,576.00**	**7,576.65**	**.22%**
421.00	Reimb Consultant Revenue	10,451.46	15,690.00	(5,238.54)	-33.39%	188,277.36	188,280.00	(2.64)	
422.00	Reimb Expense Revenue	4,634.29	821.00	3,813.29	464.47%	9,268.58	9,852.00	(583.42)	-5.92%
	Subtotal	15,085.75	**16,511.00**	**(1,425.25)**	**-8.63%**	197,545.94	**198,132.00**	**(586.06)**	**-.30%**
432.00	Sales and Use Tax	271.59	245.00	26.59	10.85%	2,945.42	2,940.00	5.42	.18%
	Subtotal	271.59	**245.00**	**26.59**	**10.85%**	2,945.42	**2,940.00**	**5.42**	**.18%**
	Total Revenue	173,679.44	**297,554.00**	**(123,874.56)**	**-41.63%**	3,577,644.01	**3,570,648.00**	**6,996.01**	**.20%**
	Reimbursables								
511.00	Structural Consultant	2,836.16	1,536.00	1,300.16	84.65%	18,435.04	18,432.00	3.04	.02%
513.00	Electrical Consultant	5,434.28	2,944.00	2,490.28	84.59%	35,322.82	35,328.00	(5.18)	-.01%
515.00	Other Consultants	43,906.00	9,396.00	34,510.00	367.28%	112,752.32	112,752.00	.32	
	Subtotal	52,176.44	**13,876.00**	**38,300.44**	**276.02%**	166,510.18	**166,512.00**	**(1.82)**	
522.00	Reproductions	3,906.20	2,116.00	1,790.20	84.60%	25,390.30	25,392.00	(1.70)	-.01%
523.00	Models/Renderings/Photos	2,653.10	1,437.00	1,216.10	84.63%	17,245.15	17,244.00	1.15	.01%
525.00	Postage/Shipping/Delivery	1,500.30		1,500.30		9,751.95		9,751.95	
	Subtotal	8,059.60	**3,553.00**	**4,506.60**	**126.84%**	52,387.40	**42,636.00**	**9,751.40**	**22.87%**
	Total Reimbursables	60,236.04	**17,429.00**	**42,807.04**	**245.61%**	218,897.58	**209,148.00**	**9,749.58**	**4.66%**
	Revenue Less Reimbursables	113,443.40	**280,125.00**	**(166,681.60)**	**-59.50%**	3,358,746.43	**3,361,500.00**	**(2,753.57)**	**-.08%**
	Directs								
601.00	Direct Labor-Principals	3,583.78	4,842.00	(1,258.22)	-25.99%	59,404.68	58,104.00	1,300.68	2.24%
602.00	Direct Labor-Employees	46,851.25	52,083.00	(5,231.75)	-10.05%	636,594.13	624,996.00	11,598.13	1.86%
	Subtotal	50,435.03	**56,925.00**	**(6,489.97)**	**-11.40%**	695,998.81	**683,100.00**	**12,898.81**	**1.89%**
	Total Directs	50,435.03	**56,925.00**	**(6,489.97)**	**-11.40%**	695,998.81	**683,100.00**	**12,898.81**	**1.89%**
	Revenue Less Reimbursables, Directs	63,008.37	**223,200.00**	**(160,191.63)**	**-71.77%**	2,662,747.62	**2,678,400.00**	**(15,652.38)**	**-.58%**
	Indirects								
701.00	Indirect Labor-Principls		149.00	(149.00)	-100.00%	1,792.00	1,788.00	4.00	.22%
702.00	Indirect Labor-Employees	1,676.00	1,543.00	133.00	8.62%	18,512.00	18,516.00	(4.00)	-.02%
703.00	Job Cost Variance	(35,277.50)	(26,612.00)	(8,665.50)	32.56%	(319,347.00)	(319,344.00)	(3.00)	
	Subtotal	(33,601.50)	**(24,920.00)**	**(8,681.50)**	**34.84%**	(299,043.00)	**(299,040.00)**	**(3.00)**	
711.00	Holiday	2,320.00	430.00	1,890.00	439.53%	5,160.00	5,160.00		
712.00	Vacation	600.00	390.00	210.00	53.85%	4,680.00	4,680.00		
713.00	Sick Leave	320.00	79.00	241.00	305.06%	944.00	948.00	(4.00)	-.42%
718.00	Business Development	512.00		512.00		2,144.00		2,144.00	
	Subtotal	3,752.00	**899.00**	**2,853.00**	**317.35%**	12,928.00	**10,788.00**	**2,140.00**	**19.84%**
747.00	Repairs & Maintenance					300.00		300.00	
	Subtotal					300.00		**300.00**	

v6.1.500 (ADMIN) -

FIGURE 1

Profit planning monitor from Deltek Vision software compares your budget with operating income and expenses for a given period as well as year to date.

49

or perhaps there's some other problem that needs to be addressed. The most important thing you can require of your bookkeeper in keeping this report accurate and useful is to make sure there's consistency in how items are identified in your books and there's a clear and concise explanation of the item being posted. Having someone post "credit card charges" doesn't help you understand the actual expense charged against that account.

CASH JOURNAL

This report is exactly as the name implies: it details the cash coming in each month and the cash going out. This is helpful in understanding your monthly cash flow. It isn't the appropriate tool to use to understand profitability, but it's the tool you can use to know if you're meeting your monthly expenses and to understand your tax position.

ACCOUNTS RECEIVABLE REPORT

This report is a simple breakdown of who owes you money from the invoices you've billed to your clients.* It's based on how old an invoice is (or "aged"), typically organized in monthly increments and determined by the date when it was mailed. Most reports show you what invoices were just mailed, and what invoices are still outstanding from the last thirty-, sixty-, and over-ninety-day cycles. This report allows you to track the problem payers and address them before they get too delinquent. Remember that the older a bill is, the harder it is to collect. Good reporting tools also show you the last payment you received from a client and for which invoice it was paid. Sometimes this feature is helpful to see if a client skips a payment. With this information, it'll be easier to address this problem.

ACCOUNTS PAYABLE REPORT

This is also an aged report that tells you to whom you owe money.* It's customary in design firms to invoice for consultants that are going to run through it's office, such as engineers. Therefore, it's

*For a sample report, visit www.thebusiness ofdesign.net.

important to understand to whom they'll owe money once they get paid by the client. Often the language in your contract addresses payment terms called "pay when paid," which enables architects to wait until they get paid by the client before they have to pay their consultants. I've witnessed on numerous occasions that when cash flow gets tight, many designers use funds that come in to help supplement their own cash flow. This is a bad practice, because if things don't quickly improve, you'll have difficulty finding the money to pay your consultants. I was once brought into a firm that needed to get out of financial trouble because it used over $1 million of its consultants' fees to fund its own bad management issues. It was a painful transition for the company and almost put it out of business, but we were able to negotiate terms to pay everyone back. It's important to never think of this as your money and to pay those consultants immediately when the cash comes in. Understanding exactly how much money you owe people helps you understand your true cash flow and manage relationships with your vendors. If you find yourself in a difficult spot, it's better to communicate your difficulties to your vendors than to have them spread the word that you aren't paying your bills. It all comes down to communication when managing relationships and expectations.

PROJECT-RELATED REPORTS

The following reports are essential to help you manage your projects from a financial standpoint.

The project progress report shows you the progress of each individual project in your office. It should detail the current time period and the project-to-date figures (the total time and expense charged against a project from its inception) to help you understand how successful (or not) these projects are for the firm. A good tool will tell you as much detail as you need or as little as you are capable of managing. The reports can often show great levels of detail, but few people are capable of actually managing that much information. The more comfortable you are with the data, the more effective you'll be in your management. What this report allows you to track is exactly who charged time to your project and what expenses are being applied to the project. It also compares the established budget with the fees you've negotiated for the project. If you see you're going off track, then this tool allows you the opportunity to correct the project's path. Without this information you're managing in the dark. Typically these data are updated weekly.

The project summary report is a summary of all the projects in your office for a given period of time. Many systems allow you to sort this report in different ways. For instance, if you want to see these data by principal or project manager, then you can see how successful all the projects under the direction of that person are and compare them with those being managed by the other people in your firm. You could also sort by project type to see what projects are most successful for the office. You may learn that one principal excels at one type of project, and it may make sense to move another type of project to someone with a different skill set. This report is valuable in understanding your project profitability from a broader perspective. If you need to dig deeper, you can always look at the project progress report for more detail.

The time analysis report tracks your staff's time by the week, month, and year. Not all software produces this information, but it's valuable to see how much direct time—the amount of billable time—your employees have for the period you're analyzing. At the beginning of each year, you should establish goals for your employees in order for them to understand what's expected of them when it comes to how "billable" you want them to be. There are standards for staff to be billable in percentages based on hours officially in the office, which are listed below. FIGURES 2 AND 3

Principal: 50 percent

Project Manager: 80 percent

Job Captain: 88 percent

Draftsperson: 95 percent

Intern: 95 percent

TIME ANALYSIS REPORT

Benson Research Lab   Retrieve Mode: All Data * ETC/JTD Date: 1/31/2011

Labor | Consultant | Expense | General | Rates | Top-down Plan | Analysis

Labor   New Row   X Delete   Insert   Employee   Generic   Search   Indent   Outdent

Description	Start	Finish	Planned Hrs	Subrow	Q3 2010 Sep 2010	Q4 2010 Oct 2010	Q4 2010 Nov 2010	Q4 2010 Dec 2010	Q1 2011 Jan 2011	Q1 2011 Feb 2011	Q1 2011 Mar 2011	Q2 2011 Apr 2011	Q2 2011 May 2011	Q2 2011 Jun 2011	Q3 2011 Jul 2011
▸ ⊟ Benson Research Lab	5/11/2008	6/25/2015	16,049	Gantt											
				Planned Hrs	554	348	413	436	367	316	360	283	283	293	268
				Actual Hrs	88.50	268.75	10.00	8.75	70.50						
				Revenue	44,532	21,306	25,941	27,495	22,395	18,441	20,877	18,576	18,576	19,026	17,676
⊟ Pre-Design	5/11/2008	9/30/2011	6,240	Gantt											
				Planned Hrs	304	64	59	63	53	50	57	16	16	18	2
				Actual Hrs	39.25	146.00	2.00	7.25	44.00						
				Revenue	27,861	1,185	702	756	702	702	756	702	702	756	
⊟ Code Analysis	5/13/2008	3/31/2011	215	Gantt											
				Planned Hrs	38	6									
				Actual Hrs	39.25	146.00	2.00	7.25	44.00						
				Revenue	3,051	483									
Jensen, Chris	4/5/2010	10/2/2010	215	Gantt											
				Planned Hrs	38	6									
				Actual Hrs	31.75	74.25	2.00	5.00							
				Revenue	3,051	483									
⊞ Programming	6/11/2008	9/30/2011	3,525	Gantt											
				Planned Hrs	174	58	59	63	53	50	57	16	16	18	2
				Actual Hrs											
				Revenue	15,216	702	702	756	702	702	756	702	702	756	
⊞ Site Analysis	6/15/2008	10/2/2010	2,500	Gantt											
				Planned Hrs	92										
				Actual Hrs											
				Revenue	9,594										
⊟ Schematic Design	7/11/2008	1/16/2011	262	Gantt											
				Planned Hrs		36	94	98	34						
				Actual Hrs	49.25	122.75	6.50	1.50	24.50						
				Revenue		2,736	7,038	7,386	2,991						

FIGURE 2

Time analysis report from Deltek Vision software analyzes the staff's billable time and compares it with the target you set for each employee.

FIGURE 3

Billable targets for different levels of staff

BILLABLE TARGETS GRAPH

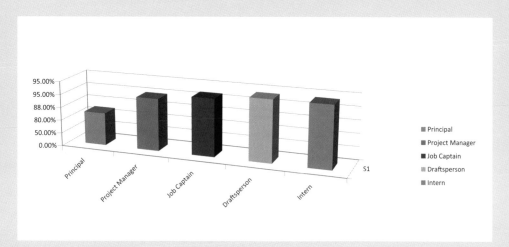

■ Principal	
■ Project Manager	
■ Job Captain	
■ Draftsperson	
■ Intern	

The standard number of hours that people work annually is 2,080, excluding overtime, and from that we deduct the amount of vacation, sick, and holiday time they've earned. For example, if you have a full-time employee working 2,080 hours and he or she gets two weeks of vacation time (80 hours), one week of sick time (40 hours), and seven paid holidays (56 hours), the math looks something like this: 2,080 - 80 - 40 - 56 = 1,904 potential billable hours. If we want them to be 90 percent billable, then their target would be 1,714 hours that we'd want them to bill on projects during the year. If their billing rate is $100 per hour, then you could budget for them to earn $171,400 for the company in a given year, based on their billable time. This doesn't take into account any overtime or time you may choose to write down for lack of efficiency or being over budget. I've found this formula useful to determine expected revenue by staff. Of course you'll need the work to make certain you have the amount of work necessary to bill this much time. (My philosophy has always been to hire first for talent, and the work will follow.)

PURCHASING REPORTS

If your firm purchases goods and services on behalf of your clients, you'll want to make sure you understand how much you've billed your client for these goods and services and how much you owe your vendors for these goods and services. For example, if you're custom building a sofa for your client, it may require five purchase orders: one for the frame, one for the finisher, one for the upholsterer, one for the fabric, and one for the trim. You'll need to get deposits from your client for the cost of each item and then keep track of each purchase order to know when the remaining balances are due. Even if the client pays for 100 percent of the piece up front, you still need to manage the dollars going to each vendor. Multiply this by the hundreds of items you're buying, and it becomes a complicated management issue. With the right reports, you can track every expense as well as how each item is moving from vendor to vendor. These reports help you manage the purchasing process. If you're

PURCHASING REPORT

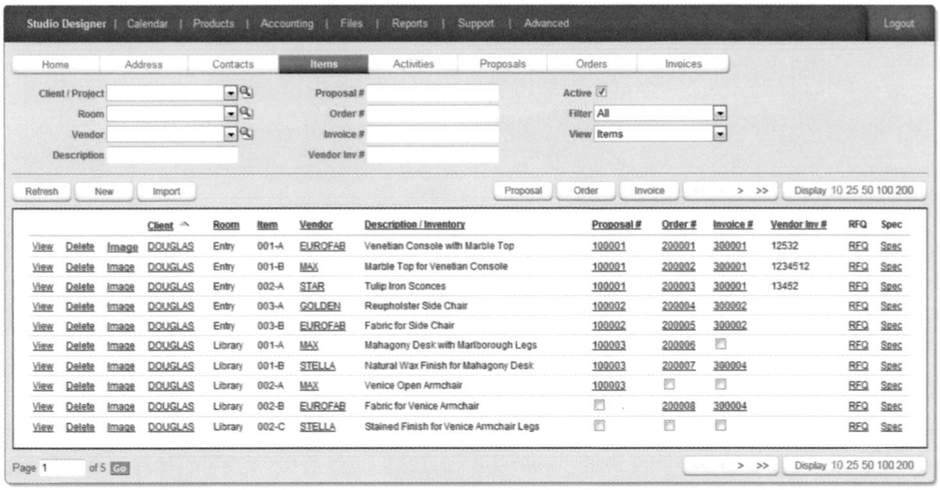

			Client	Room	Item	Vendor	Description / Inventory	Proposal #	Order #	Invoice #	Vendor Inv #	RFQ	Spec
View	Delete	Image	DOUGLAS	Entry	001-A	EUROFAB	Venetian Console with Marble Top	100001	200001	300001	12532	RFQ	Spec
View	Delete	Image	DOUGLAS	Entry	001-B	MAX	Marble Top for Venetian Console	100001	200002	300001	1234512	RFQ	Spec
View	Delete	Image	DOUGLAS	Entry	002-A	STAR	Tulip Iron Sconces	100001	200003	300001	13452	RFQ	Spec
View	Delete	Image	DOUGLAS	Entry	003-A	GOLDEN	Reupholster Side Chair	100002	200004	300002		RFQ	Spec
View	Delete	Image	DOUGLAS	Entry	003-B	EUROFAB	Fabric for Side Chair	100002	200005	300002		RFQ	Spec
View	Delete	Image	DOUGLAS	Library	001-A	MAX	Mahagony Desk with Marlborough Legs	100003	200006			RFQ	Spec
View	Delete	Image	DOUGLAS	Library	001-B	STELLA	Natural Wax Finish for Mahagony Desk	100003	200007	300004		RFQ	Spec
View	Delete	Image	DOUGLAS	Library	002-A	MAX	Venice Open Armchair	100003				RFQ	Spec
View	Delete	Image	DOUGLAS	Library	002-B	EUROFAB	Fabric for Venice Armchair		200008	300004		RFQ	Spec
View	Delete	Image	DOUGLAS	Library	002-C	STELLA	Stained Finish for Venice Armchair Legs					RFQ	Spec

FIGURE 4
Sample of a purchasing report from Studio I.T.

managing services on behalf of your clients, these reports can help you manage the percentage the vendor is reporting are complete compared with the percentage that actually are complete.

The most important thing to realize from all these reports is that they represent historical data, which means there's nothing you can do about what has already occurred, but what you learn from these reports can influence how you manage your firm and the success of the projects moving forward.

Summary reports are often created by your software, but in many cases they're created in Excel to allow customization for your firm's needs. FIGURE 4

Now that you know what reports you need to run your firm, I can show you how to review all these data. The following report we created years ago for our clients. We call it our "Executive Summary," and it'll help you manage your firm each month. It's a dashboard that can show you your financial health on a single sheet of paper. FIGURE 5

Column 1: a description of each line item

Column 2: current-period data

Column 3: the period budget

Column 4: year-to-date data

Column 5: year-to-date budget

Column 6: prior-period data

Column 7: previous-year data

First grouping of rows: income-related data

Row 1: total income

Row 2: reimbursable income less expenses

Row 3: purchasing income

Row 4: purchasing expenses

Row 5: purchasing profit

Row 6: overhead expenses

Row 7: net profit

Row 8: overhead percentage

Row 9: breakeven

Second grouping of rows: labor-related data

Row 10: net-fee income

Row 11: direct labor

Row 12: indirect labor

Row 13: effective multiplier

Row 14: staff utilization

Other financial data

Row 15: checking-account balance

Row 16: savings-account balance

Row 17: client deposits

Row 18: line of credit outstanding

Row 19: accounts-receivable balance

Row 20: accounts-payable balance

FIGURES 6 AND 7

EXECUTIVE SUMMARY

CATEGORY	CURRENT PERIOD SEPTEMBER	CURRENT PERIOD BUDGET	YEAR TO DATE	YTD BUDGET	PRIOR PERIOD AUGUST	PREVIOUS YEAR
INCOME AND EXPENSE DATA						
Total income	$635,125	$625,000	$5,716,125	$5,600,000	$612,345	$498,745
Reimb. Inc. Less Expenses	$12,307	$10,000	$110,763	$90,000	$9,809	$11,004
Purchasing Income	$429,025	$400,000	$3,807,000	$3,600,000	$408,024	$398,045
Purchasing Expenses	$330,019	$300,000	$2,935,008	$2,900,000	$300,122	$306,188
Purchasing Profit	$99,006	$100,000	$871,992	$700,000	$107,902	$91,857
Overhead Expenses	$156,003	$150,000	$1,404,027	$1250,000	$154,033	$128,909
Net Profit	$76,194	$100,000	$596,101	$900,000	$75,989	$93,180
Overhead %	2.14	2.00	2.14	2.00	2.19	1.98
Breakeven	3.14	3.00	3.14	3.00	3.19	2.98
LABOR RELATED DATA						
Total Net Fees	$305,106	$325,000	$2,656,309	$2,5000,000	$3000,456	$287,098
Direct Labor	$72,909	$75,000	$656,181	$625,000	$70,434	$65,009
Indirect Labor	$26,232	$22,000	$236,088	$198,000	$26,503	$20,989
Effective Multiplier	4.18	4.33	4.05	4.00	4.27	4.42
Staff Utilization	75.00%	78.00%	74.00%	78.00%	77.00%	72.00%
Other Financial Data						
Cash on Hand - Checking	$200,232				$305,987	$297,677
Cash on Hand - Savings	$498,002				$345,804	$502,345
Client Deposits	$1,236,708				$988,098	$709,665
Line of Credit Outstanding	$0				$0	$45,000
Accounts Receivable	1,409,504				$1,120,988	$1.190,889
Accounts Payable	$19,008				$22,119	$14,590

KEY FINANCIAL DATA QUARTER TO QUARTER

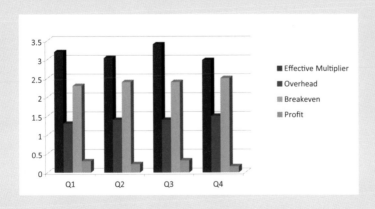

FIGURE 5
Sample executive summary report, which provides a snapshot of an interior design firm's financial health

FIGURE 6
Graph of key financial data for an architecture firm

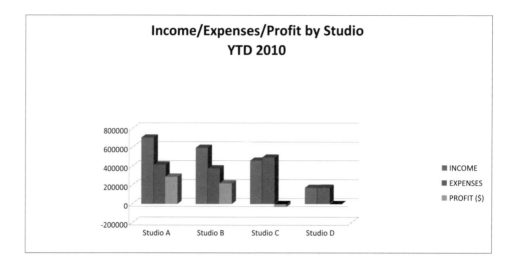

FIGURE 7
Graph comparing four
studios

ACCOUNTING SYSTEMS: REPORTS AND DATA REVIEW

As in many professions, there are software packages to help you manage your accounting needs. However, there are few comprehensive packages for our profession. Many firms use QuickBooks, but the reporting tools are not as detailed as I recommend to manage a design practice. Granet and Associates has worked with and recommended two companies for years and supports their efforts to advance their technology to accommodate the changes in our profession. Those two programs are Deltek Vision for architects and Studio I.T. for interior designers. FIGURES 8 AND 9 An example of how these companies keep expanding their offerings is the newest feature offered by Studio I.T., called Studio Market. It allows you to identify your personal inventory as a sale item that can be posted on the Studio I.T. website simply by checking a box in your inventory. All the designers utilizing this software will have access to these items. Can you imagine having access to thousands of designers' personal inventories? It allows for a designer to sell inventory purchased with a particular client in mind but never sold. Now it can be available to others by a click of a button. Brilliant.

FIGURE 8
Deltek Vision software is one of the most utilized software packages for architectural firms across the country.

FIGURE 9
Studio I.T. Inc. software is one of the most utilized software packages for interior design firms nationwide.

WHAT SHOULD YOU EXPECT FROM YOUR ACCOUNTING SOFTWARE?

The best software packages allow you to enter information once, to be spread throughout all the different kinds of reports you need.

For an architecture firm, the software should provide all your monthly financial statements, project reports, employee reports, time management reports, and budgeting and projection reports. The system should also produce your monthly invoicing and check processing. Years ago we had clients who wouldn't allow their invoices to be printed by the "system" because the Courier font didn't look good enough. I would tell them that it needed to look like a bill and not a proposal, otherwise their clients wouldn't respond to it as quickly. I know we're in an aesthetically pleasing industry, but it's fine for some things to look pedestrian if they actually help expedite the task required. And such a thing would be making your invoices look like bills so they get paid quickly. Today we can make invoices look as beautiful as we want, but I still believe they should be clearly labeled as invoices.

For interior design companies, the software should generate all of the above-mentioned reports, as well as provide you with all the reports and billing necessary to manage your purchasing functions. For instance, you should be able to enter a purchase order for a piece of furniture and track it as it moves from place to place, from the framer to the finisher to the upholsterer to storage and finally to the client's home or office.

When selecting software you should remember that only a small portion of the costs is in the software: the true costs are in training and time to get the system up to speed with your internal data. I highly recommend that you plan for how you want your system set up. This will require you to understand what end result you're looking to achieve from the data you want to analyze. Many, many times we've come into an office to reconstruct a software setup, because it was created to be much more complicated than anyone could have ever managed. If you think of this like a design project where you start out designing the general parameters of the project and then quickly understand how you or your client will use the project, it'll help you in identifying your needs. I tell my clients to set up the system only to the amount of detail they can manage. If you can manage a tremendous amount of detail, you should have a more detail-oriented system. Start with simplicity. You can always expand on the detail, but it's hard to simplify a detailed system.

HOW OFTEN SHOULD YOU LOOK AT YOUR DATA?

You should look at the data as frequently as you can, but to assist you with certain timelines, I've outlined the appropriate frequency of each report listed. Remember: the more information you can manage, the better control you'll have in running your practice. You want to be smart about this or at least smarter than the person I just read about in a newspaper whose accounting person walked off with $1.2 million. Or the client of mine who called me after the bookkeeper forgot to bill 30 percent of a client's purchasing order for a job that had been closed for a year.

Look at the information below with the following frequency.

Cash balances: weekly

Project reports: weekly for project managers, monthly for principals

Time cards: weekly

Purchasing reports: weekly

Financial statements: monthly (they should be reviewed by the second week after closing the month)

Accounts receivable: monthly

Accounts payable: monthly

Executive summary: monthly or quarterly, depending on your financial position

Accountant's financial review: semiannually

Creating a budget: annually but reviewed semiannually

BUDGETING

There are two major areas that design firms should have budgets for: annual operations and projects. Annual operating budgets help manage the running of your firm, and project budgets help manage the running of a project.

ANNUAL OPERATING BUDGETS

This budget allows you to set goals for each income and expense line item on your income statement. It always surprises me when I learn that design firms don't budget for their annual income and expenses. It's important to set goals for your firm and your employees. I recommend that when you start the annual budgeting process, begin with your staffing needs for the year, which will quickly translate into a revenue projection for your firm.

Some firms are known as "hire/fire firms" because they staff up for new projects and let people go when the projects stop. Firms turn to this method of management when they're ill equipped to manage their company. Hiring and firing on a project-by-project basis is extremely unproductive and only addresses short-term needs. It also creates an unhealthy working environment. My philosophy on hiring the right people and the work will come falls into what I call the *Field of Dreams* phenomenon: if you build it, they will come. If you know how to protect your core staff, then you know how much work you need to support that core. To create your own budget, start with your income. FIGURE 10

61

COLUMN 1: the name of your employee

COLUMN 2: the hourly cost of that employee (if he or she is paid $60,000 per year, the hourly cost rate would be $28.85, determined by dividing $60,000 by 2,080, the number of work hours in a year)

COLUMN 3: 2,080 total work hours in the year

COLUMN 4: the number of vacation hours

COLUMN 5: the number of sick hours

COLUMN 6: the number of paid holidays

COLUMN 7: the total number of hours the employee will be in the office (column 3 minus the sum of columns 4, 5, and 6)

COLUMN 8: the employee's utilization rate, which is the number of direct hours you expect an employee to work on a project for the year (e.g., 75 percent would mean that you expect an employee to bill thirty hours of a forty-hour week)

COLUMN 9: the employee's billing rate

COLUMN 10: the employee's potential revenue (column 9 x column 7 x column 8)

COLUMN 11: the employee's annual cost rate (column 2 x column 3)

COLUMN 12: the target multiplier, which is the multiple that you hope to achieve from that employee's cost rate (e.g., if you target a 3.5 multiplier, you want to be able to bill 3.5 times every dollar charged to a project); in residential design we target a 3.25 to 3.5 multiplier; in other types of design firms, we hope for a 2.8 to 3.0 multiplier

COLUMN 13: potential revenue based on your target multiplier

COLUMN 14: the difference between column 10 and column 13. (If this column is in the negative, it means that your billing rates for your staff are below what you're targeting for them to earn with their target multiplier. It also means your billing rates should be examined closely.) Also note that senior members of the staff may never be able to bill their target multiplier, because their costs are too high and your billing will not bear the burden to achieve a

CHEVIOT DESIGN GROUP

BUSINESS AND FINANCIAL MANAGEMENT

EMPLOYEE	COST RATE	HRS	VAC	SICK	HOL	POT HRS	UTIL	BILL RATE	POT BILL	COST	TARGET	POT REV	DIFF
Adams	$41.35	2080	80	40	56	1904	0.95	150	$271,320	$41.35	3.50	$261,779	$9,541
Andrew	$60.25	2080	160	40	56	1824	0.5	250	$228,000	$60.25	3.50	$192,318	$35,682
Bley	$29.57	2080	80	40	56	1904	0.95	125	$226,100	$29.57	3.50	$187,202	$38,898
Bliss	$48.08	2080	80	40	56	1904	0.95	175	$361,540	$48.08	3.50	$304,385	$12,155
Davis	$24.98	2080	80	40	56	1904	0.95	125	$226,100	$24.98	3.50	$158,143	$67,957
Eserts	$22.12	2080	120	40	56	1864	0.9	125	$209,700	$22.12	3.50	$129,880	$79,820
Green	$27.88	2080	80	40	56	1904	0.95	125	$226,100	$27.88	3.50	$176,503	$49,597
Joshua	$60.25	2080	160	40	56	1824	0.5	250	$228,000	$60.25	3.50	$192,318	$35,682
Kaufman	$33.00	2080	80	40	56	1904	0.8	125	$190,400	$33.00	3.50	$175,930	$14,470
Nelson	$45.08	2080	120	40	56	1864	0.9	175	$293,580	$45.08	3.50	$264,692	$28,888
Swiller	$43.27	2080	80	40	56	1904	0.9	175	$299,880	$43.27	3.50	$259,516	$40,364
Vaszauakas	$31.25	2080	120	40	56	1864	0.9	125	$209,700	$31.25	3.50	$183,488	$26,213
TOTAL									$2,925,420			$2,486,152	$439,268

FIGURE 10
Tool to calculate potential
revenue for your annual
budget

3.5 multiplier. The company should be able to achieve its overall target because of junior staff earning a significantly higher multiplier, averaging out the firm's target, which is typical.

Once you've established your targeted income, you have to evaluate if you think it's realistic for the income you anticipate receiving. Many people will lower it by 10 percent to set a reasonable target for the firm. Keep in mind that this formula doesn't take into account any overtime billed.

Now that you've determined your income from fees, you need to determine other anticipated income. You should budget for reimbursable expenses, purchasing, and consultant expenses that come from consultants who are billed as reimbursable to your clients. The best way to determine these numbers is to look at historical data and determine what percentage this represents of your total income in the past.

After you project your income you need to determine your expenses for the coming year. At Granet and Associates we typically break expenses into three categories: reimbursable expenses that run through your firm; direct expenses that are not reimbursable but are included in your fees, such as consultants; and operating expenses, which include your rent, insurances, marketing expenses, office supplies, and so forth. Many of your expenses will be fixed, such as rent, salaries, and insurances for the year, and you should use the actual amounts when creating your budget. For the discretionary expenses, such as marketing, bonuses, profit sharing, office supplies, and computers, you should create a budget for each line item. It's important to work with the person you plan on holding responsible for these expenses. This assures accountability by allowing him or her to help author the budgets.

Once you determine all of these expenses, you can then input your budget and determine if it creates the level of profitability that you desire. If it's too little, then you need to work the numbers to determine where you can cut your expenses. If your salaries are too high, you have two choices: cut staff or find more work for the staff. If your profit is unreasonably high, then you may want to look at your spending and determine if you've adequately provided for the expenses needed to maintain the level of revenue you're projecting.

Budgets are powerful tools for tracking how you're performing in comparison with how you anticipated you would perform at the beginning of the year. Our clients aim to achieve 20 percent profitability. That being said, we have clients whose profitability ranges from 8 percent to 40 percent, depending on their practices. A typical profit percentage for our clients is 20 to 25 percent of total billings.

PROJECT BUDGETS

Project budgeting is the process of understanding the fees that you negotiated for a particular project and then breaking those fees down into the project's phases. In architecture this includes schematic design, design development, construction documents, bidding, and construction administration. In interiors it may include the same phases, but you might add purchasing/expediting as well as installation. Installation can be a significant percentage of your fees, and you should allocate the appropriate dollars to that phase.

Once you determine your project fee, I recommend you take 10 percent of the fee off the top for a contingency. My philosophy is that if you give people $1,000 to work on a project, they'll spend $1,000 or maybe even $1,200. The contingency allows for your staff to target for a healthy project or to accommodate unanticipated expenses.

With the project fee determined and split by phases, you then want to determine who's working on each phase of the project in your team. It's not necessary to determine specific people but roles that each person is performing: for instance, the principal-in-charge, the project manager, the job captain, the designer, and so on. In my experience, for every ten firms, you'll see at least five different titles for the same position. Once you determine the fees assigned to each person, you should communicate to all team members what time has been allocated to them for a particular project.

I'm always amazed when principals are reluctant to share project financial information with employees. The more information you share, the more employees can help manage the project and ultimately the firm. I had a client once tell me to give out only the number of hours each person had to work on a project because they "didn't need to know the dollars." I told him people don't relate to the difference of spending 100 hours or 120 hours, but they understand the difference between spending $1,000 versus $1,200. They manage their own money and expenses, and they know what it means to spend more than you have. If you give them hours to manage without the dollars, they truly cannot be invested in managing the project.

Once you have a budget for the fee portion of the project, you then need to budget the expenses. Since you've determined the labor expenses through designating the team, you now need to focus on expenses incurred on the project. These might include any consultants that you hire under your contract to help with design. It may include expenses that are both reimbursable and nonreimbursable. Examples of both of these include travel, meals, printing, and miscellaneous other expenses directly associated with the project.

Now that the budget for your individual project has been created, you can input it into your accounting system to allow it to be monitored regularly. We advise that you have your project manager monitor the budget as often as the data are updated. Our recommendation is to update the data weekly. More information on how to use your budget for effective project management can be found in chapter 5. (SEE PAGES 156-63)

CONTRACTS

Why are contracts so important? Like employee handbooks, they protect you when something goes wrong. The world would be a better place if contracts weren't necessary or if we could draft agreements that simply and clearly stated what both parties promise to perform rather than outline penalties for when and if one or both parties don't perform. But unfortunately contracts are needed for when and if something does go wrong. You need a contract that's not too complicated for every project and every client.

NEGOTIATING FEES AND FEE STRUCTURE

I remember when I first started my business. The hardest thing for me to do was establish a billing rate for my services. I had no real sense of my value from a billing standpoint. I remember approaching my first client with an agreement, and I told him that I would charge $50 an hour, which in 1991 terms was low. He said to me, "You're worth more than that. I'm going to pay you $75 an hour." And that's where I started.

Some clients love hourly billing, because they know what they can expect. Other clients hate it, because they don't want you to have an open checkbook to bill all your hours no matter how inefficient you are. I understand both sides of the argument. But in the end you should be paid for the value you bring to the table. The true negotiator knows how to express his value to clients in a way that they understand what it is that they're paying for. The following are examples of some common billing methods.

ARCHITECTURE

1 Percentage of construction. The cost of construction is the baseline for your fees. For example, if you were building a $5 million house and your fee was 15 percent of the construction cost, then your fee would be $750,000.

This method can be challenged by many clients. The most common challenge I hear is, "Why should I pay you a percentage of what the house cost? If I use marble countertops instead of tile, why are your fees dependent on the amount of money I spend on finishes?" The counterargument is that the percentage billing methodology is a barometer for the amount of fees needed to give clients the full services they should expect from their architect. Determining fees on drywall doesn't add up to much, but on hand-plastered walls it does. The amount of detail required in one case versus the other can be significant. The point here is that you can't pick apart every item and say whether the fee is appropriate. You must look at the project as a whole to determine what's appropriate.

If a client hires a respectable architect, he or she should be providing services appropriate for the fee structure negotiated. If the client feels that the fees are unfair, then unless you explain your position in a way that builds trust, this will always be an issue throughout the project. The other point to remember is that the client always has the right to approve all the expenses, and therefore your fee is not simply based on expensive finishes that the client never requested.

If you choose to bill this way, the most common way to invoice is monthly, based on the percentage completed of the project. These are the typical percentage breakdowns by phase of construction:

Schematic design: 20 percent

Design development: 25 percent

Construction documentation: 30 percent

Bidding: 5 percent

Construction administration: 20 percent

With ever-changing drawing technologies it becomes important to make certain that the effort you're putting forth on a project matches your fee schedule. For instance, with building information modeling (BIM), a significant amount of effort goes into the early stages of design (schematic design and design development). This creates a major adjustment to the construction documents and construction administration phases. We've seen the schematic-design and design-development phases increase from 20 percent to 25 percent and 25 percent to 30 percent, respectively.

FIGURE 11

It's important to bill your clients at the completion of work at the end of each month. Some firms invoice at the completion of the phase, and many months can pass before you complete a

Apple & Bartlett, PC
Architects and Engineers
100 Cambridge Park Drive, 5th Floor
Cambridge, MA 02140

Mr. John Bovis
562 Cherokee Road
Suite 500
Alexandria, VA 24578

September 09, 2010
Project No: 1999009.00
Invoice No: <Draft>

Project   1999009.00   ABC Plaza Study
Study conducted on new site. Design proposal and Site survey performed according to contract #A3299-443.
<u>**Professional Services from June 01, 2010 to June 30, 2010**</u>

Fee

Estimated Construction Cost	1,000,000.00			
Fee Percentage	20.00			
Total Fee	200,000.00			

Billing Phase	Percent of Fee	Fee	Percent Complete	Earned
PreDesign	10.00	20,000.00	50.00	10,000.00
Schematic Design	15.00	30,000.00	10.00	3,000.00
Design Development	25.00	50,000.00	0.00	0.00
Construction Administration	50.00	100,000.00	0.00	0.00
		Total Earned		13,000.00
		Previous Fee Billing		0.00
		Current Fee Billing		13,000.00
		Total Fee		**13,000.00**

Reimbursable Expenses

Reproductions	247.64	
Shipping	149.44	
Total Reimbursables	**397.08**	**397.08**
	Total this Project	**$13,397.08**
	Total this Invoice	**$13,397.08**

FIGURE 11
Sample fee invoice from
Deltek Vision software

phase; this has the potential of putting the firm at risk from a cash flow standpoint and a client expectation standpoint. Clients like to know what their monthly bills will be during the project, and if they don't receive something for several months, the bill is always a surprise and tends to require further explanation, which slows down the payment cycle.

For cost of construction design fees, the industry averages look something like the following (depending on the project's size):

Commercial: 7 to 10 percent (retail on the lower end, high-end office on the higher end)

Institutional: 5 to 12 percent (schools on the lower end, health care on the higher end)

Residential: 10 to 25 percent (depending on your client base and firm recognition)

Hospitality: 3 to 15 percent (megaresorts are on the lower end, boutique hotels on the higher end)

The following is a list of billing methods most commonly used:

❶ HOURLY: Billing for every hour you work. This method may protect you in an unstable economy. The reason clients like this is that they feel that they can track the time you're spending on their projects, much like attorneys or accountants, but what can also happen is that they want to scrutinize every hour being spent. You may hear them say, "Why did it take you five hours to work on my bathroom?" or "Why am I being charged for your staff to spend an hour on running prints?" You truly don't want that level of scrutiny for your bills, but you're open to it if you bill this way. I recommend that on your bill you show only job titles and not individual names. I also recommend that you list the amount of hours for that title on the bill without detailed backup. If clients require the backup, you always have that available for their review.

The most important thing required of you and the client in this type of billing, and for that matter any type of billing, is trust. If you have trust, these issues simply do not get in the way of doing the job you were hired to do.

② HOURLY, NOT TO EXCEED: Billing hourly is hard enough, but then you throw in the not-to-exceed part, and you're asking for trouble. The client only wins in this arrangement, because if you go over the not-to-exceed, you're required to eat your fees. If you're under, then you leave dollars on the table. Usually when a client proposes a not-to-exceed, which by the way I call "not-to-succeed," he or she has a budget in mind. I suggest you establish that budget and turn it into a lump sum fee. That way, if you're efficient, you have the chance to be rewarded for your own efficiency.

③ LUMP SUM: A lump sum method for billing can be rewarding if you understand the scope of the project and the proposed time frame. Calculating your fee can be difficult, especially since you're being asked for a fee before you truly know the client. In my opinion the best solution if this is the choice billing method is to bill hourly in the early phases, and then once the program is determined, you convert the project into a lump sum fee. That way there are fewer unknowns, and you can draw from this early experience to determine the appropriate fees. The way you bill with this method resembles percentage of construction, except your fee is fixed throughout the project.

If you choose this method, you should clearly define your scope and the timeline for the project, to allow for billing additional services if either of these elements expands. This is a good method when you've done a similar project, because you should have all the data necessary to determine a healthy fee. The only unknown becomes the new client.

④ COST PER SQUARE FOOT: In this fee arrangement, the cost of your design fees is determined by the project's total square footage multiplied by a fee per square foot. This is a rare method for residential architecture, but it's common in commercial architecture. The nice thing about this fee structure is that if the size of the project increases, your fees increase as well. The hardest part of this fee type is to determine an adequate fee based on your client and level of difficulty of the project. Sometimes the complexity increases but the square footage doesn't, and then there's the chance your fees won't cover the work required. In the case when you're repeating a design or a similar design of a previous project, this fee can be appropriate and easy to determine.

INTERIOR DESIGN

All of the above methods can apply in interior design projects, but there are additional methods of billing.

1 Markup on the purchase of furniture. Most designers mark up the purchases they make on behalf of their clients. If you ask ten designers, you probably will get ten answers, but the industry average we see is 35 percent. This figure stems from the fact that most showrooms will give a designer a 50 percent discount off the list price, who could then mark it up 35 percent, and the designer's client still saves 15 percent. Since most clients can get access to most of the goods designers have access to, this method of billing comes into question. However, what separates clients from designers is not so much the ability to find furnishings as it is the way you put everything together.

The resistance to billing on a percentage of purchasing that most interiors designers get is similar to the resistance architects get on percentage of construction cost billing. "Why do your fees go up if I purchase a $2,500 table or a $10,000 table?" This goes back to the fact that the cost assumes the value of the knowledge and talent of the designer—you hope your designer is buying furnishings appropriate to the project, and, similar to construction costs, the owner always has final approval before you make the purchase.

Another area that concerns clients in regard to this billing methodology is in understanding the true price of the furnishings you're providing. If you keep an open book, it's simple for a client to audit purchases. It'll keep you out of trouble and prevent trust issues. The one issue that you want to protect in an open book situation is your sources. You don't want a client contacting these sources directly. If you ever run into a case such as this, that's simply a bad client.

A couple of tips on selling clients furnishings that come from your personal inventory: these may be items that you've collected through the years. It's important to make it clear to your clients that you're selling to them out of your inventory at your price. If they don't agree with this price, you don't have to sell that item to them.

Another point to consider is how to charge for custom-designed products. If you consider these pieces as original works of art, it's difficult to imagine that each part of the piece marked up would be equal to its value. What I'm trying to point out is that this original piece is much more valuable than the raw cost of the item simply marked up. As Aristotle said, "The whole is more than the sum of its parts." An analogy I like to tell designers is that when you buy a pair of shoes, you don't ask how much the leather cost and how much the heel cost and how much the labor cost, you simply are told what that pair of shoes costs, and you decide if you want it for that price.

OTHER FINANCIAL CONTRACTUAL TERMS

Billing for reimbursable expenses: often when negotiating contracts for my clients, I'm asked by the client why it's important to charge a markup or administrative fee on top of the cost of reimbursable expenses. This clause is often negotiated out by designers, but when I explain to the client that the fee is there for a good reason, more often than not they accept it. The explanations I give the clients are as follows: (1) the use of your money during the period from when you purchase the item until you get reimbursed for it; (2) the cost of running expenses through your accounting system by inputting them, billing them, and collecting them; (3) most companies pay business taxes based on their cash receipts or total income, and these expenses are included in that calculation; (4) your errors-and-omissions (E&O) insurance, which is necessary to protect you against any claims made for your mistakes, is based on total income, and this expense is part of the calculation for your insurance and affects your premiums. If you add up all of these expenses, the 10 to 15 percent most people charge is not adequate.

There are other contracts you'll have to manage in your design business. Without going into great detail, it's important to understand that you may have to deal with the following contracts in your business.

Real estate leases: If you plan on renting space, you'll be required to sign a lease. There are many real estate books to explain what you're obligating yourself to in a lease.

Equipment leases: Some firms prefer to lease their equipment, because it becomes obsolete so fast or because they don't have the cash flow for large capital expenses. The typical equipment that firms lease includes computers, telephone systems, high-production copy machines, and printers, as well as large software packages.

Insurance policies: The following policies are important to have while running a design practice.

1. E&O/Professional liability. This covers you for your design and production work for your errors and omissions on your projects.
2. General liability insurance. This covers the contents of your office, including theft, fire, damage to your office contents, if someone is hurt on your premises, and lost business because of acts out of your control (not acts of God, however). It can also include coverage for automobiles that the company leases or owns.
3. Employee practices insurance. This covers you from claims for wrongful termination or any other employee claims against your company.
4. Key man insurance. This covers your firm if key employees become disabled or die.
5. Health insurance. Most firms offer their employees health insurance coverage. In some cases the typical health plan can be expanded to cover eye care and dental.

6. **Workers' compensation.** This insurance is state mandated, to cover your employees if they're hurt on the job.

MANAGING PROFITABILITY

Profitability is not what's difficult for many businesses; it's *managing* the profits that can be challenging. I'm a strong believer in sharing the wealth. I remember that M. Arthur Gensler once told me that at the end of the day if there's money to share, the receptionist may be the first to get a bonus and he would be the last. However, if there's a lot of money, the receptionist is probably going to get the same bonus, and he'd receive considerably more. The thinking behind that philosophy is that the people most responsible for bringing the dollars to the bottom line should be the ones who get the lion's share of the profits. However, since receptionists have little effect on how the company is run, then they should be rewarded for how well they're doing their job, and that probably has little to do with the amount of money the firm makes. I've always believed in that policy, but I've chosen to take that advice a step further, to create a bonus program focused on performance.*

An important note about managing profitability is to understand your tax consequences. You want to make certain that you're getting the most out of any bonus distribution. In some cases, it makes sense to pay your employees versus paying taxes to the government, but this advice should come from your accountant.

When distributing dollars for bonuses, profit sharing, or other extraordinary expenses, you must always take into account your cash position. Many companies get in trouble by distributing too much cash and not creating a cushion for the leaner times.

*Further explanation of my bonus plan recommendation can be found in chapter 4, page 125.

TEN PERCENT RULE

In the world of design it can be difficult to make money when you get started. I've always believed that if you apply these 10 percent rules, you'll get into good habits of managing your money.

1 **TEN PERCENT IN SAVINGS.** When you receive a client's check, take 10 percent of the funds and immediately transfer it to a savings account. This may not seem like a lot, but over time it'll grow, and you'll have a nice savings account by year's end. If you bill $1 million a year, you'll have $100,000 in savings if you follow this rule. We spend what we have, and if you don't have these funds in your operating account, you tend not to spend them. This can also be a cushion that can protect you for extraordinary expenses or year-end taxes.

2 **TEN PERCENT OF YOUR FEES.** When budgeting your projects you should take 10 percent off the top of your fees. This again follows the philosophy that you spend what's given to you, and if your project managers see only 90 percent of their budget, they'll manage the 90 percent.

3 **TEN PERCENT STAFF RULE.** Unlike former chairman and CEO of General Electric Jack Welch, who says you should let go of the bottom 10 percent of your staff each year (I do believe there's some good in that advice), I say you should find ways to improve your staff by 10 percent. This includes methods of educating, mentoring, and training them to perform their jobs more efficiently and to expand their capabilities.

How you treat the financial and management piece of your business sets the tone for all that you accomplish in your design practice. This is the lifeline of your business, and like your heart, if it beats regularly, everything else has the ability to perform at a higher level.

"You can avoid reality, but you cannot avoid the consequences of avoiding reality." —AYN RAND

KEITH GRANET: I heard you speak about the ownership transition program at SOM. When you are considering new future partners, it seems to me that you are not only looking to the next generation down but maybe even two generations out—people in their thirties and their forties, not just the ones with whom you've worked closely for twenty years. In reality, transition may be very quick, but the cultivation of that transition has been a methodical long-term process.

JOHN MERRILL: I think that's a key point. You always want people coming in at the lower levels, if people are leaving at the upper levels. It's written in SOM's articles of partnership that a partner has to retire when he's sixty-five. In a couple of cases, for special reasons, partners have stayed on a couple more years as consulting partners.

This sounds pretty hard-boiled, but it has done a couple things for us. The partners are not forced to make a decision about an individual partner's retirement. This partner can stay on; this partner has to leave. At the same time, it forces the partner when he's in his late fifties, early sixties, to begin to think about his retirement. He can't indulge in wishful thinking about staying until he's eighty years old. Most importantly, it indicated to the younger people in the firm with partnership aspirations that they weren't going to be blocked by a bunch of old fogies at the top. Those were the positive things. The negative thing was a lot of people are almost at the peak of their career when they're sixty-five. You lose their talents and experiences when you'd like to have them stay.

KG: Do you tend to lose any clients when partners retire? Or are many of your clients sixty-five or older at that point anyway?

JM: It's interesting; my experience is that as I got to be in my sixties, my clients were all in their sixties. They were beginning to turn over the reins of their firms to younger people. Those younger people were particularly interested in talking to the same individual in our firm that their predecessors had.

KG: So that transition has happened even at the client level.

JM: I think that's largely true. Generally speaking, we find that our clients talk to people close to their own age.

KG: Let's discuss the importance of understanding the financial structure of your firm. Is it important to SOM that designers understand the financial side of the business?

JM: Yes, when we get a project we sit down with the design partner, managing partner, and project partner and work out a budget. After the project begins, the design partner or senior partner would get a printout showing how many hours they had left. They knew exactly where they are. The system worked well.

KG: Have you seen the face of architecture change over the years? Is it a more difficult practice than it used to be?

JM: I think that there has been a significant change in terms of client relationships, a general deterioration of the practices. I don't like to be somebody who thinks in the past, but I recall in the fifties and sixties that the relationship between client and architect was very close. You were friends; contracts were three pages long. If there was a problem, things would be settled by sitting down with a client and working it out. There was not the litigious atmosphere that exists now.

KG: Speaking of clients, what do you think makes the perfect client?
JM: I'm trying to think of some perfect clients. I've had some pretty good ones. One of the best corporate clients I've ever had—I won't mention his name—had a major company with which he had strong family ties. This building [that we were designing for him] was really more than just a building to him. It was going to be a headquarters office building, and something he wanted to be proud of.

We were talking about a new concept of interior layout. He went to Germany to look at all the places that had that layout. When he came back, there was a lot of resistance among his senior management, because this was a new idea. He sold them on it. He was totally involved all the way through.

He certainly would be the perfect client. There are a lot of other kinds of clients. A developer-client, for example, is going to be a different kind of person.

KG: Is the ideal client educated in the architectural process, yet leaves you alone to do what you do best?
JM: I think if he is educated architecturally, or at least aware architecturally of good design, it makes your job an awful lot easier. I think important qualities are an awareness of what is good architecture, somewhat of an understanding that the process is about understanding that you need to pay your architect to get from here to there, and being reasonable and fair. If you've got that, you've got a good client.

KG: Speaking of people's work, who influenced you when you were in practice? Whose work did you admire?
JM: Well, I had a unique education, because I went to Minnesota for two years, then I went to MIT. I think a lot of my generation was very interested and influenced by Bauhaus and Philip Johnson at that time. There were also the usual people in the forties and fifties, which was the International Style, although I did work with Bill Wurster.

KG: Do you think architecture, like most fields in art, needs to be in your blood; you just have to have this love for it?
JM: I think if you're going to be a "design architect," yes. When I was eight or nine years old, I was drawing floor plans of houses. Architecture is so diverse that other people pursue it for other reasons. They're interested in the technical side of architecture. They like the idea of helping to build something. I don't think everybody has to be of the mind-set, "I want to design the most beautiful buildings in the world." Others can say, "I'd like to help put these buildings together."

KG: How would you like to be remembered as an architect?
JM: I would like to be remembered as an architect who served as a catalyst between those very talented design architects that I've worked with and the people in the office who contributed to the projects and the client. One who contributed to the quality of his projects.

CHAPTER 3

Marketing and Public Relations

If finance and business management are the lifeblood of your company, then marketing and public relations are its voice and face. Being the best-kept secret in our business is not a great idea. Many people equate it with exclusivity, but in truth you can be exclusive yet known for your work at the same time. Life is easier when people know who you are. When clients know your work, they'll come to you rather than you always chasing them; when potential employees know about you, they too will seek you out because they know your work. When talent is in rare supply, you want these people calling you rather than you spending time and dollars on recruiting. Vendors, consultants, and peers who know of you will be able to refer business to you when projects come to them first that they know are appropriate for your firm.

Many people ask me the difference between marketing and public relations. Marketing is the research and pursuit of work available in the marketplace. Public relations focuses on exposing your firm to as many targeted people as desired. It can be outreach to shelter magazines, bloggers, trend articles, or any other source to introduce the firm to the audience you seek. To be successful at either of these efforts, you need to have a strategy. In marketing it may be how many past and new contacts you're going to target in a given time frame. In public relations it might be the number of projects you'll get photographed and published in the same time period.

MARKETING

One lesson I learned years ago while at Gensler—and one that I cannot emphasize enough—is that you need to market and get your name out there when you're the busiest. This is a hard concept for people to grasp, because they're fearful that they won't be able to handle any more work when they're busy. It seems hard to believe that you should seek new work when you're in the thick of designing and building your projects. But if you think about the lead time required to bring in new work—usually several months ahead of when you'll be billing a good portion of the fees and keeping your staff busy—you can quickly understand that if you wait until you "need" the work, it's too late. The timeline may look something like the following illustrations (depending on the scope and size of the project). FIGURES 1 AND 2

It takes a couple of months to be courted by a client, another month to negotiate the contract, and then a couple of months to get through the project's early stages (concept, schematics) when someone other than the principal and maybe one other person is working on the project. Add that up, and it can be five months before you're actually working on the project. So it's important to always be looking for work.

For those firms that have built a great reputation and are highly sought after by clients, they may have the luxury of telling

TIMELINE

FOR BRINGING IN A NEW PROJECT

Initial Contact for a New Project (WEEK ONE)	
Research potential Client	Prepare Materials for Interview

Meet with Potential Client (UP TO THREE WEEKS)	
Send Proposal	Set up Next Meeting

Negotiate Terms (UP TO FOUR WEEKS)	
Review with Insurance / Attorneys	Draft Negotiated Agreement

Set up Kick-off Meeting (UP TO FOUR WEEKS)	
Meet with Client	Predesign Services

Begin Project (UP TO THREE WEEKS)	
Project Budgets and Planning	Begin Schematic Design

**Process Can Take Anywhere from 12–20 Weeks
Before You Are Able To Invoice a Client**

FIGURE 1
Process for attracting,
interviewing, and landing a
typical project

MARKETING PLAN/TIMELINE

CA Create Awareness	DM Direct Marketing
Website, Blog, Social Media	Mailers, Postcards, Newsletter, Email Blasts
Project Signage	Regular Email Updates
Charities	Holiday Mailer
Professional Organizations	Social Media Updates
Referral Network: Brokers, Clients, Contractors, Design Professionals	Business Cards
Public Relations	
Client Maintenance	

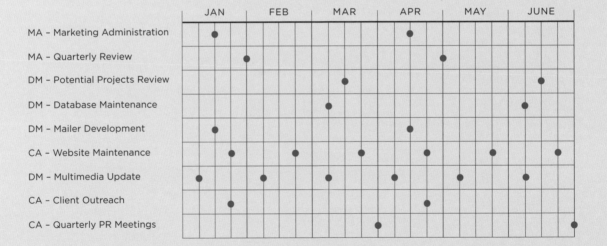

FIGURE 2

Annual marketing plan with timeline for frequency of activities

TM Target Marketing	IP Interview Process	PM Promotion Marketing
Portfolio Packages	Project Portfolios	Photography, scouting, completed work
RFQs, RFPs	Final Photography	Aware Submissions
Speculative Work	Firm Profile	Email Project-Completion Assessment
	Relevant Project History	Internal Office Display
		Media Outreach

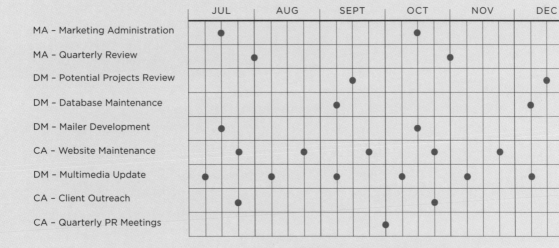

a client when they can start work on a project. This gives them the necessary backlog not to worry about where the next project is coming from, but this is more the exception than the rule. I must say the client who's willing to wait is rare, but he does exist.

But how much backlog does a firm need? It depends on the type of work and projects your firm seeks. Backlog is defined as enough work to keep your firm busy during a certain period of time—usually six to twelve months. This is the combination of new prospects that you're more than 75 percent certain will turn into projects and the active projects currently in-house. If you have a solid six months of backlog, you can weather most storms.

Another question that I'm often asked is who markets for the firm? Most people think that the principal and partners do. For the most part they're the most adept at this role, but the truth is, if you're smart, you'll teach every employee to market for your company. If people are proud of where they work, they'll talk about it, and you never know when that talk will reach a potential client.

I experienced this firsthand as a twenty-two-year-old office assistant at Gensler. One day I was riding the bus into San Francisco on my way to work. Sitting next to me was a woman who asked what I did. I told her I worked for an architectural firm named Gensler and Associates. She said, "You know I know of Gensler because you guys sponsor *Masterpiece Theatre* on PBS. However, that's all I know about the firm." I told her that we specialized in high-end interiors for big corporations and law firms as well as many other project types. She was the secretary to the managing principal of a leading law firm in the city, and her boss had recently told her that their lease was up, and they'd need to find new space and an architect to design it. She asked for a business card. I guess you know where this story is going. Gensler got the job, and it was a fairly major project for the office.

When I tell this story, people always ask me: "What did you get for bringing in the project?" I joke that I got to keep my job. The truth is there was no direct compensation for bringing in the work, but there was great pride in doing so. In staff meetings Art

Gensler would announce new projects and where they came from, and you wanted to be on that list. I also know that somewhere it paid off in my bonuses and advancement in the firm.

Gensler had a strong culture, and marketing was an essential part of it. An initiative at Gensler was to place employees on the board of directors of a nonprofit company to have a more active role in the community. Any organization could be chosen, because Gensler knew if employees were interested in something, they'd get involved. I was interested in theater, so I was placed on the board of the One Act Theater in San Francisco to lend my financial skills to preparing the theater's annual budget. At one board meeting the director asked if anyone knew of an architect who could help with remodeling the theater. I think you get the point.

From airplanes and grocery-store lines to cocktail parties, it's all about being willing to talk about what you do and be proud of it. People react positively to those who feel passionate about their careers. Many people have called me the "great connector." It's part of what I love doing, whether it's about putting clients together to collaborate on a project or finding an employee for a client or a product development manufacturer for a licensing deal. It's all about who you know and how to marry them with the right synergy that works for all involved.

BUILDING A MARKETING PLAN

The success of your marketing plan depends on how comprehensive it is and how viral it can become. That is, you want to create a plan that not only spreads the word but keeps your audience coming back for more. The more someone is exposed to your company, the easier it is for him or her to give or bring you work. Think of it as that Breck commercial years ago that said, "If you tell two friends and I tell two friends and so on and so on." The word spreads much faster, and if done correctly, it can be somewhat effortless. The following tools are all part of a comprehensive marketing plan.

FIGURES 3-6

PUBLIC OUTREACH

An outreach program allows you to connect to your community. The more people who know about your firm, the more chances you have that one of those contacts will lead to a project. The following are some examples of public outreach that I believe will help you gain exposure.

❶ PUBLIC SPEAKING. Look for opportunities to communicate your message. This could take the form of giving a lecture, participating on a panel, or teaching a class. When I started my business, I looked for organizations that were related to my business and spoke about what I did for similar companies, and it always resulted in at least one new client. Of course, I was less picky then about whom to take on as a client, and I'll talk about this later in this chapter.

This approach is effective because when you're speaking in front of any group of people, you're seen as an expert in your field. Of course, you need to have something compelling to say to attract a potential client, but you're halfway there if you're standing in front of a potential group of clients. For example, I have a New York client who was eager to find work in Los Angeles. She's a high-end residential designer, and she was asked to speak to the Bel Air Garden Club. This audience was filled with people who love design, who usually live with beautiful gardens, and who therefore usually have wonderful homes to go along with those gardens. If any of them were looking to remodel their home, the chances of them being in the audience were very high. This is exactly how she attracted a new client from that particular event. The project is significant, and the effort is modest in comparison with the potential outcome.

Another reason to speak is to attract good talent to your firm. When the economy is robust, one of the most difficult challenges is to find the right people for your firm. In a strong economy, the talent available to you becomes limited. The more you speak at schools and events, the more exposure you'll have to the labor pool.

2 **GETTING INVOLVED.** Another lesson I've learned through the years is how important it was for my firm and for my own personal growth to get involved in the community. Whether it's joining a board or a committee, or just getting involved in community activities, it introduces you to many different people whom you'd otherwise not have the opportunity to meet. It's easy to go to work, go home, go to work, go home, day after day after day. It takes effort to get involved, but it's an effort with great rewards from the people you meet and the exposure to different environments.

3 **CHARITIES.** Using a portion of your gross revenues to develop a philanthropic effort is both good business and good for your soul. Being able to help organizations with a mission that's close to your heart is a wonderful thing. It's also important to understand that philanthropy can be a source of exposure for your company to potential work. If you give, you get. That's simply the way it works. You should never give to get. But if your mission is pure, you do get back in return.

FIGURE 3 Website for Appleton & Associates, a good example of a clear, easy-to-navigate architecture website

FIGURE 4 Website for Rios Clementi Hale Studios, a good example of a dynamic website that allows the visitor to easily access the full breadth of the work of this multidisciplinary firm

FIGURE 5 Website of Ferguson & Shamamian Architects. The site immediately tells you who they are and the work that the company designs. It's also accessible, compelling, and beautifully displayed.

FIGURE 6 Website of Victoria Hagan, a simple and beautifully displayed example of this firm's work that captures its essence

4 **OTHER COMMUNITY ACTIVITIES.** Some of our architect clients have served on planning boards or even as planning commissioners. Others have been involved in local or national organizations such as the American Institute of Architects (AIA). We had one client who as president of the national AIA received calls for potential work from foreign entities simply because he was president. What's important to remember is that you need to have a true interest in the organization you join for it to be successful. If it's not a true interest, then you won't be fully engaged and it won't generate work. No matter what your choice of organization is, it's all about attaching yourself to your interest. If your choice of organization is a Harley motorcycle club because you own a Harley, then you'll be surrounded by like-minded people who probably have similar interests. Chances are that they own their own homes, own their own businesses, and if you're one of the few if not the only designer in the group, the opportunity to get work will be high.

FIGURE 7
Although somewhat obsolete, the business card still remains a valuable tool to share contact information and create a dialogue with prospective employees, clients, and colleagues. It's also a way to quickly communicate your aesthetic.

⑤ NETWORKING. People who exude passion about their careers talk about their work at parties, on airplanes, or wherever they can. I'm not proposing that you walk around preaching your business, but I certainly know that when you're proud of your work and you talk about it, people can hear the excitement and enthusiasm. That's a part of what inspires them to consider you for a project they may be thinking about. The only caveat is that if your passion is not matched to the recipient's level of interest, it may not be well received. Skilled marketers know when to bring up an idea and when to talk about a project because their radar is up and they understand that the receiver will in fact be interested. It takes three parts perception and one part chutzpah to land a project.

All of your employees should have business cards. Make it easy for them to be contacted by a prospective client or employee or vendor. Cards may be obsolete, yet we all pass them out. They're visual and convenient, and until everyone can simply zap their information to one another, we still want them. FIGURE 7

AWARENESS
This portion of the plan is devoted not only to creating awareness but also to the ongoing need to keep your visibility high at all times.

❶ POSTPROJECT COMMUNICATIONS. Most people don't understand the importance of reconnecting with clients after a project is completed. I think some of this comes from fear that you don't want to hear all the problems that clients are experiencing with their projects. But clients like it when you keep in touch. Designing a home or an office builds a very personal relationship, and oftentimes there's separation anxiety at the project's end. If you remember that most successful businesses are based on having a high repeat-client base, then it makes sense to care for past clients. The fear of not wanting to know about the problems is actually a lost lesson: you can learn from the mistakes of the past. Clients who know you care are more forgiving when you want to help them solve their problems than the clients who get ignored. One of the most important reasons to keep in touch with your clients is that if you have regular contact with them and a new project comes into play, you'll be the first person/firm they think of to give the project.

Remember: it's about who you know and who knows you. Most projects come to the people who are connected to the owner and not the people who blindly submit a portfolio in hopes of getting the job. Many projects are awarded before anyone ever knew there was a project.

2 **REPEAT BUSINESS.** At least 85 percent of your work should be repeat business. As you first start out, this of course won't be possible, but for well-established firms, you should count on the majority of your business coming from longtime clients. What I mean by "repeat" is that it's either a client coming back for another project or a client has referred you to another potential client.

Some of our clients have patron clients. These clients come back year after year with new work. They involve you in each of their homes or in each new project they're developing. Our favorite ones we like to call "serial builders"—people who always have to have some project under construction at all times.

Patron clients can be the most wonderful clients to have. The relationship and trust is deep, and there tends to be great respect. Yet it can also be problematic if the boundaries get blurry. If you forget that you ultimately have a business relationship with your clients and you then become friends with them, you have to be careful about how you handle your business terms.

One of our clients has a high-end residential practice that would never have been able to compete in the institutional market if it weren't for a patron client, who made a significant donation to endow a building at a major university. Today, with this building in the portfolio, our client can compete with great confidence.

3 **WEBSITE.** Your website is a vitally important place to build awareness in your community and client base. It's the first place someone will visit after or even before talking to you. Your most current work should be posted, along with your press and enough information about your firm to intrigue a possible client. Because this may be the first place people look to see if you're the appropriate designer for their project, it should speak to your aesthetic. It must be graphically pleasing, not too wordy, and easy to navigate. It's still true that a picture is worth a thousand words.

4 **JOB SIGNS.** This may seem like a simple thing, but you'd be surprised at how many people don't post their firm's signs at a job site. Passersby are curious about projects under construction, and if they're interested in the design and your sign is up, you're making it easy for them to reach out to you.

CREATING COMMUNITY

The purpose for becoming part of a community is simple: it allows for your vision to be shared and for others to care about your success. A community allows for others to take an active role in the growth and success of your firm. This can lead to new projects, new employees, and a shared responsibility for your welfare and the welfare of the other community members. FIGURE 8

Chandelier by Fontana Arte, Fred Silberman

Plank-top table by Silvio Coppola, Donzella Ltd

Thad Hayes'
Six Quick Picks
from *1stdibs*

1940's Royere Day Bed, Magen

Massive Stoneware "Mountain Pot" by Michael Arnzt, Fat Chance

Eames Child's Chair, Mark McDonald

Philippe Hiquily "Quilles" table, Liz O'Brien

FIGURE 8
A view of the Style Compass section of the website 1stdibs.com featuring the designer Thad Hayes. This demonstrates alternative ways to market through nontraditional media outlets.

I find it curious that the design community is often anything but a community. We have so much to share that would help strengthen our industry, yet there's very little transparency about how we run our practices. I've made it my mission to improve how the design industry conducts itself as a business. The more we share information with each other, the stronger we become as a community. It's a career mission—if I'm instrumental in planting and germinating the seeds to build a healthier community, then that may be enough to start a movement that will grow well beyond my career.

What does it mean to create a community? I define *community* as a group of people who are all involved for the common good within a single environment: they're working to create social cohesion within this environment. Each one has its own individual strengths. They can be competitive with each other, and they can also be collaborative. The difference is that they understand the power of sharing, of shared resources and shared knowledge.

To this end, I cofounded an event called the "Design Leadership Summit." It was formed to create community among the thought leaders in design. Each year it grows, and each year we learn the community's needs and try to address them by bringing in experts from other industries to explore alternative ways to grow and manage our participants' businesses. What has come from this unique gathering of leaders is a place to share ideas and to find resources to support each other. Working relationships and support systems have formed between the group's members that don't exist within our industry.

This is the true meaning of community, bringing together people from different skill sets and allowing them to realize the strength of their collective talents.

So how do you build a community that can aid your personal growth and professional outreach? Clearly there are organizations you could join, such as the AIA and the American Society of Interior Designers, but I believe that's simply one piece of the building process. Another way to build a community is to seek out people willing to share their interests and support your interests and who also can provide you with a different perspective for your environment. Your community should consist of the following groups:

1. Other design professionals within your specialty
2. Other design professionals outside your specialty
3. Resource-related professionals, such as lawyers; accountants; business consultants; and banking, investment, and insurance firms
4. Schools and institutes that provide resources for talent
5. Vendor resources, such as contractors, suppliers, and manufacturers
6. Professionals who can potentially supply you with work, for example, real estate agents and developers
7. End users of your products, that is, if you have a practice that designs restaurants, then get to know the restaurant owners and make them a part of your community

Once you identify the people who belong in your community, it's not enough to simply know them. It's much more involved and complex, because the greatest asset of the community is the relationships. Like any good relationship, a community takes work to nurture and sustain. You need to engage and invest yourself in the relationships of that community to actually make it work for you.

"The perfect client makes you a better designer." —*VICTORIA HAGAN*

Creating a community may seem elementary and obvious, but where it tends to fall down is in the maintenance and growth. The most important aspect of creating a community is the understanding that giving for the sake of giving is far more effective and rewarding than giving for the sake of getting. If you put something out in the world for the right reasons, it'll come back to you in the most unexpectedly rewarding ways. This isn't to say that you can't be purposeful in your outreach. Anything done for the good of *only* one party is never good for either party.

FINDING A NICHE

To help separate you from all the generalists in the marketplace, you should find a niche. It allows for you to develop an expertise in a particular aspect of the design profession and for people to be aware of your particular talent.

Once you find your particular talent and nurture it, clients will select you because of your expertise. If I'm looking for an airport architect, I will probably only consider designers who have that level of expertise. Although designers have gotten work because a very creative client was willing to take a risk on a firm that didn't have the exact experience he or she was looking for, that's very rare.

So how narrow does your niche have to be? It needs to be narrow enough to articulate your expertise in the project types you're skilled at. Another way to define your niche is to create an aesthetic "look." This look will define you, such as Frank Gehry's work for the Walt Disney Concert Hall (2003) or the Guggenheim Museum Bilbao (1997). A signature style helps build a brand and communicates a clear message that's easy to express to your potential client base. But a signature look is not always the key to success, and we have many clients who don't have a signature look. They call it a "reverse ego" because they're providing their clients with a design that's unique to them, not to the designer. There are probably more of these types of firms in the world than those with a signature look. My point here is to emphasize why you need to communicate who you are and why a client should hire you. It's easier if your message is clear, and it's critical that you learn how to articulate your message.

LEARNING HOW TO SAY NO

If you can achieve a certain level of success where saying no is more common than saying yes, this will be a powerful place for you to be during your career. There's great power in saying no, yet it's a difficult concept for designers to understand. It mostly comes from fear. Fear that you never know where that next project is coming from, fear of alienating a potential client, and fear in believing that no matter how much you think the project isn't right for your firm, it just may grow into something bigger and better in the future.

The most important decision-making element is your gut reaction to a client/project. Always listen to that feeling. It's there for a reason, and I know whenever I've ignored the feeling it comes back to haunt me.

The following are questions to ask yourself before taking on a new project or client.

1. Do I like the client?
2. Will this project advance my goals for the firm?
3. Can I work with the client?
4. Does the client appreciate my expertise?
5. Does the client have the proper budget to build this project?
6. Are all the members of the team people I can and want to work with?
7. Have they offered me a glass of water?*

*I put this in to see if you're paying attention, but the truth is that if a client doesn't offer you a glass of water, or anything for that matter, that client probably doesn't care about you. This may seem harsh, but I've tried it, and it's true. The client needs to treat you right for any project to be successful.

If you can't answer yes to all of these questions, you need to say no to the project. Some people will tell you that if you can answer yes to six out of the seven, then you should take on the project (or if you desperately need the work, you should say yes, no matter what). I'm here to tell you that you should never say yes unless you can say yes to all of these questions. If you take on the wrong project for what you think are the right reasons, then when the right project comes along you'll be too busy with the wrong project to see it. A bad client, a bad team member, a bad budget are all ingredients for disaster.

You'll notice that not one of the questions refers to your fees. This is because your fees should not be the main factor in deciding to take on the project. Start with the questions above, and you'll have the answer to your fees. If clients truly appreciate your work, they'll pay for it. If your fees represent value to them, they'll pay for it. If clients sense that you don't appreciate your own value, you'll never be able to justify your fees.

Many people ask how small residential practices eventually move on to work with major corporations: such practices have learned to say no to the wrong projects or clients, but they've also learned that residential clients can be a great source of new business opportunities if they simply ask. I don't think Robert Stern or Michael Graves would've had as many opportunities without Michael Eisner, or Philip Johnson without real estate developer Gerald Hines. These relationships and their respective trust were deep. What may have started out with small-scale projects grew into large-scale, world-class projects because of that trust.

PUBLIC RELATIONS

PR for design firms is typically handled by professional agencies with expertise in the design profession. One of the most significant ways PR agents earn their fees is in knowing when trend stories are slated to come out and how to put their clients out there as experts. They can also be useful in assisting you to strategize the right image you want to present to the public.

The PR process can take years to develop. You may have projects ready to be published, but are the publications ready for your projects? Most publications schedule issues far in advance, and knowing that information is important to time your outreach to the magazines. You should expect to wait a minimum of six months from the time your project is presented to getting it in a magazine. There are shorter time frames, as well as longer ones, but most magazines have a backlog of projects, and just getting slated for a particular issue takes time. Many of the most published designers did not achieve success overnight. They worked hard to build relationships with editors to show that their design work was worthy of publication.

When we first started working for one of our clients that receives great press, people asked me all the time who handles her PR. She does. When you have a successful design practice, magazine editors will approach you to talk directly to the source. If you can forge those relationships within the publication world, then you'll have the press knocking on your door.

It's always my recommendation, whether or not you have a PR agency, to reach out and get to know the key editors in our business. The web is the place for great exposure through blogs and social media sites. There's no ignoring the importance of this vehicle as an outreach tool.

Designers want to be in all the shelter magazines; it's also desirable to appear in magazines that your clients read. When you visit their offices, pay attention to the magazines and newspapers on their desks. If you work a lot with attorneys, try to get one of your law office projects published in the *ABA Journal*. You'll be the only designer profiled, and the target audience is perfect. Some of the best magazines are lifestyle magazines that clients read more of than industry publications. Magazines like *Departures*, the publication for platinum card holders; *Town and Country*; *Vogue*; the *Robb Report*. Some of the airline in-flight magazines are good, because you have a captive audience, especially on long flights when there's nothing else to read. Publications such as the *Wall Street Journal*, the *New York Times*, and other major city Sunday magazines almost always focus on design, and their large circulation results in terrific exposure.

Another item to consider in getting published is to hire photographers who work closely with the magazines. If you like a particular photographer and he or she is often published, hiring that person to shoot your project gives you another in at magazines to approach about getting your work published.

The public relations portion of your marketing plan should include the following elements.

1 THE RIGHT PR AGENT.

a. Make certain they have specific industry experience.

b. Get recommendations from present and past clients.

c. Ask for recommendations from editors to understand the relationships agents have with the editors of the major industry publications.

d. Look carefully at their client base to determine if they know your specific world.

e. Get a comparison of at least two agency contracts.

f. Make sure they are the right fit for you both from how they will represent you and how you will work together.

g. Make certain they are savvy in all aspects of media, print, web, social media, and television, if that is important.

h. Look at the longevity of their clients: if they have short-lived relationships, they probably get hired for short-term assignments and don't build long-term PR relationships.

i. Go with your gut: if it feels right after all your research, it is probably right; if it does not feel right, it probably is not.

Understand how much you can afford to pay. Most qualified PR firms charge a monthly retainer.

This is a very social profession, and you always want to make certain you and your PR firm know what's going on in the industry. It's important to get a list of events worth attending that

FIGURE 9 Holiday cards are an important way to connect with your clients each year.

FIGURE 10 Granet and Associates tenth anniversary piece, designed by David Lecours. The band holding ten thank-you cards expressed our thanks to our clients for their support and also asked them to use the enclosed thank-you notes to thank the people who were important to them.

attract both clients and peers who will bring exposure to your firm. If you're not in a position to hire your own PR firm, it's important that you follow these recommendations and try your best to make yourself present in the community and get to know the important connections in the press. FIGURE 10

2 DIRECT OUTREACH. This is the establishment of a program that allows your firm to gain exposure through your ability to reach people with all forms and methods of communication.

a. A graphic representation of your work: A regular mailing—a minimum of six times a year—puts you in front of your existing and potential clients. Graphic representations of your work can include, for example, a postcard (a beautifully designed graphic that illustrates a project) or an email blast that can attract attention. An email that says "look at our work" will probably wind up in a spam folder. But if it's an email that tells a story, solves a problem, or simply just inspires someone, then you've reached your audience.

b. A holiday mailing could be a card but doesn't necessarily have to be the holiday you're thinking about. We had a client one year who mailed a deck of playing cards for Valentine's Day, and it was very clever and came as a surprise to everyone. Many people create a New Year's message. The significance of these pieces is to make people take notice of your firm. A holiday card has the potential of getting lost among hundreds of others sent at the same time. If you want to send a message at this time of the year, send one that'll be noticed. Our firm sent out a holiday card printed on beautiful rag, because we didn't want to kill any trees, and we later noticed that it decorated many desks for months after the holiday, because people simply liked it.

FIGURES 9 AND 10

3 SOCIAL MEDIA. What is social media and why is it important to the design community? The key word here is *community*. Social media refers to the community we establish online with others.

our powder room before and after

about me

GIANNETTI HOME
Design Online

Many of you have inquired about
my design services and ordering
furnishings that I show here on
Velvet and Linen. We now offer
online services. To find out more
click here or contact me directly at
bgiannetti@mac.com.

**SUBSCRIBE TO
VELVET AND LINEN**

Enter your email address:

[Subscribe]

Delivered by FeedBurner

FIGURE 11 Velvet and Linen blog. This blog developed by Brooke Giannetti demonstrated a quick way to reach thousands of people interested in the design profession. This media outlet is growing in value to our profession daily.

Facebook, Twitter, Myspace, blogs, websites, and even iPhone applications can all be forms of social media. I've seen a design blog post a product on its pages, and the retailer will be sold out in a matter of hours. It's about outreach and how far and fast you can spread the word. It's about letting people know that you exist beyond the traditional methods I've highlighted in this chapter.

Although social media is a potent way to communicate, it's essential to understand that there's little or no control over the content of this type of media. You're at the mercy of the blogger, unless you're the author and can put the right information into the hands of potential clients. My warning is simple: be mindful about what you put out in cyberspace.

I often wonder who has the time to read all the information posted on the internet, yet it's gained huge traction. In the design world, blogs are popping up all the time. If you know the author, you tend to pay more attention to what he or she has to say. We have a client who started a blog, and in a very short time she had eight thousand hits a day—that's a very large audience. FIGURE 11

The ability to find information in today's world is both astounding and overwhelming. **Rutherford D. Rogers, a Yale librarian, said, "We are drowning in information and starving for knowledge."** This is even more evident with our access to information. My belief is that it isn't about how much information you have or even how much knowledge you gain from all this information, but what wisdom you can attain from all of this content.

4 AWARD SUBMISSIONS. Winning awards can be very satisfying to you as a designer, as well as to your employees and clients. The award itself is a nice recognition of the work you do every day, but the acknowledgment from your peers and industry professionals is what's most rewarding. It's another form of outreach that puts your name on the marquee. Clients like to know that their designers are successful and that they're appreciated within the industry.

Create a list of awards offered for the type of work you do. Make certain you understand all the requirements of these awards, and create a schedule to deliver submissions on time. Be selective about the work you're submitting. If you truly don't think it's your best work, you should reconsider the value in submitting the project. Oftentimes these submissions are put up for public display; if it's not your best work, consider the message you may be sending the viewer.

If you're trying to gain experience in a new project type, often unbuilt work that was part of a competition can be considered for awards. This is a way for you to gain recognition in a new expertise.

5 PUBLISHING A BOOK. Publishing a book either of your work or of a certain methodology of design can create awareness of your design aesthetic and point of view. The importance of having a book of your work is similar to being able to speak to an audience: you're held up as an expert on the subject matter. It gives real credibility to your work and can be a helpful tool in marketing your work. There are many things to consider in publishing a book, and I can't possibly give you all the ins and outs of book publishing in this chapter. Instead, I'd like to give you a list of questions to help you determine when you may be ready to publish your first book.

a. Do you have something unique to say?

b. Has your work developed enough that you believe it should be memorialized as a book?

c. Is there an audience for your book? Who's the audience?

d. What other books in the market appeal to you, and do you want your book to be similar?

e. Who will write the book?

f. Do you own your photography? This can be one of your greatest expenses.

g. What publishers are most appealing to you?

h. Do you think a publisher will acquire this book, or will you self-publish?

i. Do you know whom you'd like to hire to design the book? If not, research potential book designers.

j. If you self-publish, do you have the resources (money) to complete this project?

"In order to be irreplaceable one must be different."—COCO CHANEL

KEITH GRANET: Can you point to any characteristics that distinguish your firm from other design firms, in the business sense?

A. EUGENE KOHN: As a firm we have tried to maximize the quality of the building within a client's budget. That is, in every detail, quality of materials, quality of space that comes through that we are trying to give them their money's worth. To do that, you don't play it safe. There are some architects who say, "Look, I don't want to redraw one line, so I'm going to play it safe." They make decisions that they know will come in under budget. We try to say, if the budget is x dollars a square foot, everything we do to maximize that amount is for the client, yet make the most beautiful building.

KG: If clients had a greater social responsibility to their buildings, fluctuations in the economy would be mitigated, and their environment would be enhanced. You would have buildings and environments that are healthy.

EK: You need to realize that what you build is not something personal. It's not like buying your own car: you park it in your garage; it's yours. When you build a building, it has an impact on people long beyond your lifetime. If it's an eyesore, it stays there. People are depressed by it. Designing buildings is a great responsibility. It is a responsibility that you have to shoulder.

What drives most buildings is the user, not the owner. If the users were all better

educated, if they said, "My city is important, my environment is important; I'm not going to rent in a disaster that's been built cheaply," we'd all be better off. If the users were more selective and felt strongly about issues other than just pure cost, then the developers, the corporations, would build better buildings.

KG: So you are saying that there's a lack of concern for a long-term contribution to a community, a lack of desire to give back to society?

EK: There are some people who do give back. David Rockefeller happens to be one of them. He is the exception, not the rule. We designed a building for him at the end of the eighties, which never got built because of the market. A prospective tenant came to him for the whole building, but wanted to change the design somewhat in order to make it adapt to their needs. David loved the building so much, he refused. I admire that, because most developers say, "What do you want me to do, I'll change it." We were ever willing to make changes, but David loved the design. That kind of client is rare.

KG: I think architecture is perceived more as a luxury than it is a necessity. Your motivation for going to an architect is different than that for going to a doctor or a lawyer.

EK: You go to doctors and lawyers out of fear. You're afraid for your life; you're afraid of being in jail; you go to your accountants because you're afraid of the taxes. Those professions help you to protect yourself. They are perceived as helping to solve problems. In contrast, people are afraid of the architect. They're afraid that their money is going to be spent foolishly, that they're going to go broke. We are viewed as somebody they can't truly rely on or trust.

KG: Do you think there is an answer to that?
EK: Yes, we have to be more professional; we have to be better as businessmen. When we're done we need to be able to show that our building produced more return because it was built from a superior design. However, it's a catch-22, because to be better at what we do, we need to get the appropriate fee.

KG: And to get the right fee we need to support each other as professional colleagues.
EK: To do that, the AIA has to become a leader.

KG: How would you identify an ideal client?
EK: The ideal would be someone who has the ability to financially give us the time we need to investigate, which we do a lot. One of our best clients is this elegant family man, somebody you would be honored to have as a friend and as a business associate. Decisive, honorable, has the money to pay you, will pay you, and does pay you. He has good taste. If he says they're going to do it, they do it. That's a good client. They care about their staff. They realize what they do represents their company. Our best clients pay us; I keep stressing this because a lot of clients don't.

KG: Many of my clients who have started their own business have been sidetracked
by the amount of time managing a firm requires. They have been sidetracked from the thing they love: design. How do you feel about that?
EK: When we started the firm, we were sensitive to that. Each partner needed to, one, worry about projects first. Two, we each had individual responsibilities, called collateral tasks: financial, business, hire and fire, social. That's the way it's worked. I tend to be the one that's more outside with clients, attending the social events and charitable events as well as giving speeches. Bill Pedersen talks more about design; I talk about both design and the firm. Our role is social responsibility. Every one of us can talk about a building's aesthetics, a building's technology, and yet we can also talk about the management of the firm and the marketing. I think it's important. It's something we set out to do and we've done it.

KG: Who inspired you, in the beginning, to be an architect?
EK: There were two. Paul Rudolph was the first and Louis Kahn was the second. I studied with both. They made architecture truly exciting for me. Those two if I were to pick.

KG: How would you like to be remembered as an architect?
EK: Good question. I never thought about that. I want to be remembered as an architect, not as a marketer or a designer that worked in management. I try to be an architect who believes very much in the value of what we do as architects in society; therefore, the importance of architecture to people's lives. So I want to be remembered as somebody who really cared about the society through my professional contribution as an architect.

CHAPTER 4

Human Resources

I've found that some people simply forget that the design business is essentially a service business. Except for the designers who sell products, most of us design something on paper that someone else will ultimately build. We need to remember that the two most important aspects of running a service business are ❶ our staff is our number one asset and ❷ how we treat people is the most significant part of protecting that asset. Whether it's how you treat your employees or how your employees treat each other, or how you and your staff treat clients and how the clients treat you, it all sets the tone for your practice. If you surround yourself with people trying to build a career rather than just having a job, you'll both be mutually served.

Human resources is the key to a successful practice. You can't have a successful practice without understanding the value of the employees. You can have all the documents and manuals in place that tell people you care about them and their growth, but if you don't practice what's in those manuals, they won't matter one bit.

We write many employee manuals, but the best manual should have only four words in it: "Simply use good judgment." If people would understand those words before reading a manual that tells them how to behave, the employment world would be much easier to navigate. Every employee manual ever written was written for one reason, to protect the firm from that one person who doesn't use good judgment or simply wants to break the rules. There are important aspects of employee manuals: you should be very clear about benefits, policies, and job descriptions, but it should never be used to police your staff.

I've learned many lessons through my years consulting as well as my years as an employee. One lesson I learned very early on was about how important communication—acting quickly and responsibly if something just doesn't seem right—is to the growth of your staff. This lesson stems from my first ninety-day review as an employee. Gensler had hired me to run the mailroom. I took my job seriously and quickly found ways that the company could save money and put systems in place that helped me advance to other tasks in the company.

But my review was anything but positive. My supervisor was the manager for the San Francisco office. The first words out of her mouth completely shocked me. She said, "Keith, I don't think this is going to work out." I was devastated. I loved my job and I loved the firm. The problem was that I talked too much. I asked her how long this had been bothering her, and she said from the first day I started at the company. She thought I was talking too much, but in fact I was telling the people I delivered the mail to what was in their mail to help them address it more quickly.

It didn't seem to matter: her mind was made up and I had to go. Not knowing what to do, I asked her boss, who was the managing principal of the office, to sit in on the rest of the review. He liked me because I also delivered his mail. He told her that I wasn't going anywhere and that I was doing a good job.

I tell you this story because the lesson is very simple: you need to communicate your concerns immediately and not wait for ninety days or longer till it's time for someone's review. Reviews, I teach my clients, are for goal setting and not for punitive actions. Punitive actions should happen the moment a problem develops.

If you take the time to connect to your staff, your clients, your consultants, then you build relationships. Having relationships with people is ultimately what keeps them around. I often hear people say, they stole my best employee or my former employee stole my best client. Employees and clients cannot be stolen. They went somewhere else because they had a relationship with that person. If you lose these people, it's you who failed to maintain these relationships.

How do you build relationships? Without getting into all the psychology of human behavior, I'll tell you the secret I've discovered: it's all about being a good listener. In the design profession 80 percent of our job is problem solving, and if you know how to listen, then you can help people solve their problems.

There are two types of listeners. **Those who listen to listen and those who listen to react.** People who listen to listen are truly engaged in what you're saying, and they respond to your thoughts in a way that allows you to feel they've heard what you're saying. If you're someone who just reacts, you should slow down and ask yourself, during the conversation, whether you're really listening, and when the person makes his or her point, you should acknowledge what you just heard. Saying things like "I agree with your thoughts" or "I think you make a good point, and I'd like to tell you how I think I'd approach the situation" will keep your partner engaged in the conversation. I bring this up simply because in design if you don't design for your clients' needs but for your needs, you won't be as successful. Yes, there are people known for their formulaic design, and clients come to get exactly what those

YOU WERE BORN WITH TWO EARS

AND ONE MOUTH

THEREFORE YOU SHOULD

LISTEN

TWICE AS MUCH AS YOU

SPEAK

FIGURE 1
A valuable lesson on the
importance of listening

designers have to offer, but that's a rare minority. When it comes to design products, you have to design with the end user in mind. FIGURE 1

If you remind yourself to ask, "Am I listening to listen?" then you'll be engaged with your partner and the relationship will begin to form. The firms with the most successful track records are the ones whose people know how to listen, and through their listening they understand how to manage their clients. The most successful firms also realize the importance of communication, even if they have to communicate bad news. People prefer honesty over cover-up. You'll build a stronger relationship by acknowledging your mistakes.

There are many relationships you'll have during your career: employee to employer, employer to employee, designer to client, designer to consultant, designer to vendor, and designer to manufacturer, to name a few. The most likely place you'll start is employee to employer or vice versa.

Whether you're hiring your first employee or your tenth, or you're the employee being hired, it's crucial to hire first for fit and second for skill. The right employee has both these traits. Many people believe that skill is most important and that if the new hire doesn't completely fit in, it'll be no problem. I believe otherwise. The chart on the next page is a tool I use to hire a new staff member as well as to evaluate my current staff. FIGURE 2

The x-axis represents culture, or how a person fits within your organization in terms of his or her personality. The y-axis represents skills that he or she possesses, adjusted for relative experience. The diagram is divided into four quadrants. The bottom-left quadrant represents the low end of the spectrum—someone with low skills and low cultural fit—these people should not be in your organization. The top-left axis represents a person with strong cultural fit but low skills; the bottom-right axis represents someone with a strong skill set but low compatibility. Everyone in the top-right quadrant has high culture and high skill. This is the quadrant that you want all of your employees to be in. It's rare, however, that you'll find all of your staff in this quadrant.

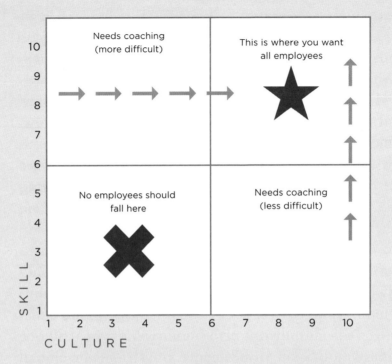

FIGURE 2 Culture/ Skill chart, first phase: understanding each quadrant

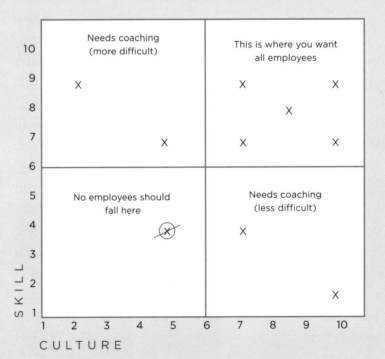

FIGURE 3 Culture/Skill chart, second phase: evaluating your staff

I've said that the staff in the bottom-left quadrant should be let go, but what do you do with the people in the upper left and bottom right? Those who fall in the upper left and who get the culture of your firm could be coached to help them improve their skill set (and move into the top right). The people in the bottom right are highly skilled, but they just don't fit in that well. People who fall in the bottom-right quadrant are far more difficult to coach, since it's an incompatibility issue based on personality.

I use this tool to help firms evaluate their staff. A lot about the firm's culture is revealed in where the majority of their staff falls on the chart. The firms whose staff mostly lands in the upper right are typically successful and high performing. Firms whose staff mostly falls in the top left tend to be sweatshops. They hire people for their qualifications, not their fit. These firms tend to produce a lot of work efficiently, but since the employees are not very synergistic, they tend to stay by themselves, and the work product tends not to improve as rapidly as with employees who work well together. Firms with most of their staff in the bottom-right quadrant tend to get along well but get very little accomplished. They love working together, but they tend not to be as successful.

During economic downturns in our industry, this tool can be particularly helpful in evaluating whom to retain. This is hard, because when you're forced to lay off staff, you often are forced to lay off people you really don't want to lose. This tool helps you evaluate the right people to keep. FIGURE 3

FINDING THE RIGHT FIT

How do you select people for your organization? At Granet and Associates, we find the following questions helpful during the interview process.

1. Why does our firm interest you?
2. How familiar are you with our work?
3. Do you know anyone who works here?
4. Why are you leaving your current employment?

5. Does your employer know you are leaving?

6. What would you say are your greatest strengths?

7. What skill set would you most like to improve?

8. Are you neat or organized? (There is a difference!)

9. Have you ever been told anything about your work that surprised you?

   Both positive and negative?

10. Do you see this as a job or a career?

Here are a few tips for reviewing résumés:

Always check references.

Avoid people who move around a lot unless you know and understand why and it makes sense to you.

If you find a typographic error on their résumé, it says a lot about their thoroughness.

The résumé is usually a good representation of who a person is. If it's neat, the person is probably neat, and if it's hard to follow or not consistent in format, the person is probably not very organized.

Whom they've worked for in the past says a lot!

Remember this is a visual profession; their résumé should demonstrate their desire to express their understanding of the importance of visual communications.

REVIEWING YOUR STAFF

Unfortunately, many firms don't review their staff regularly. I recommend that you review your employees annually and check in with them quarterly. Check-ins may simply be a fifteen-minute conference. If significant issues come up, then you'll want to extend that time to address the issues.

Annual reviews should be more formal. There should be a good form that both you (the reviewer) and the person being reviewed should fill out.*The questions you want to ask revolve around how you want this person to improve and grow in the upcoming twelve months. You should evaluate his or her skills and

*For a sample report, visit www.thebusiness ofdesign.net.

116

talents, and you should find ways to expand his or her contribution to the firm. You should also revisit previous reviews to assess how much improvement has been achieved in the past year. You should evaluate the previous goals that you set together and determine the success of those goals. The following questions are for your employees to answer.

1. What are your goals for the next twelve months, and how can the firm help you achieve those goals?
2. If you were the principal of this firm, name three things you would change.

There are two important variables about reviews: first, when to have the review, and second, who should be in the review. Some firms like to have all their reviews at once and pick a time of the year to conduct reviews, such as December or June. It's easy to experience review fatigue when you do it all at once. But some people think that if you have a staff of twenty-four, you're potentially reviewing two people every month, and it seems you're always in review mode. My preference is on the anniversary of the employee's hiring date, but either way is fine.

As for the second variable, the person who reports directly to the person being reviewed should be there as well as a senior member of the staff. There's no need for the principal to review everyone in the office. I often hear principals say it's the only time they get to sit down with certain staff members. It's a luxury for the principal to review every single member of the office, but in most cases the principal is too removed from the staff member's work, and the review will actually not be as productive as it could be if the immediate supervisor conducts the review.

Lastly, when you have reviews, people usually want to know whether they'll be getting a raise. The problem with doing this at the same time is that during the entire review the person being reviewed is thinking about the money and tends not to be focused on the review. It's better to structure the process so that the expectation is not a salary review but a performance review and that after the review you'll follow up with a salary adjustment. That way you can use the data from the review to assess salaries.

MENTORING YOUR STAFF

One of the most powerful tools for successful firms is their mentor programs. Mentoring works because it allows people the ability to grow and for the staff to know there's greater potential within the firm as long as they're growing. If you care less about their growth and more about your firm's growth, you'll compromise the firm's future. As I mentioned earlier, your staff is your greatest asset, and you need to nurture that asset to work well for you. The most successful offices are offices whose turnover is low and staff improvement is high. I mention both of these things because an office with low turnover but no growth indicates complacency—people are happy to just do the same thing as long as they have a job. That's not a healthy environment. You need both growth and stability to run a successful practice.

One of the best ways to mentor is in the art of delegating. A favorite tool of mine (from the book *The One Minute Manager*) is the Direct/Coach/Support/Delegate chart. FIGURE 4

The phases of delegation, as demonstrated in this chart, start in the Direct Box and move clockwise until you reach the Delegate Box. The Direct Box is the phase at which you need to specify, in detail, every aspect of what you're delegating. I equate this phase to when you call someone's home, and a child answers the phone. When you say, "Is your mom home?" the response is often a simple yes. You have to explicitly ask, "May I speak to her?" In this phase you have to be completely clear with everything you ask someone to do for you. I call this phase "unconscious incompetence": you don't even know what you don't know.

After you understand what they know or don't know, you get to move to the Coach Box. At this phase you're coaching them on what to do with the task you're delegating to them. This means saying things like, "Keep up the good work, but I would change x,

PHASE ONE

DIRECT	COACH
DELEGATE	SUPPORT

PHASE TWO

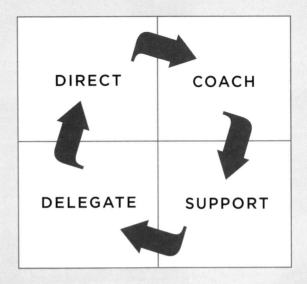

DIRECT	COACH
DELEGATE	SUPPORT

PHASE THREE

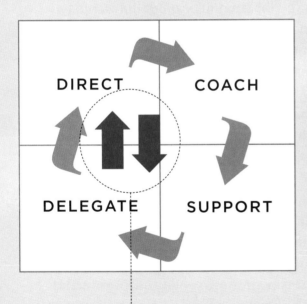

DIRECT	COACH
DELEGATE	SUPPORT

"If you don't do this, it will come right back to you to do over."

PHASE FOUR

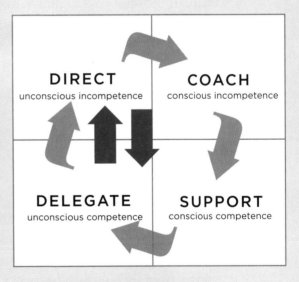

DIRECT unconscious incompetence	COACH conscious incompetence
DELEGATE unconscious competence	SUPPORT conscious competence

FIGURE 4
FIRST PHASE: understanding each quadrant
SECOND PHASE: understanding how the flow of delegation works
THIRD PHASE: understanding what happens when you ignore one or more phases
FOURTH PHASE: description of each phase of understanding
Inspired by "Coaching Stages" from Kenneth Blanchard and Spencer Johnson, The One Minute Manager *(La Jolla, CA: Blanchard-Johnson, 1981).*

y, z," or "That's OK, but you might want to change it this way to better communicate your thoughts." You're coaching this person to handle the task in a manner you want them to perform the task. We call this phase "conscious incompetence." You now know what you don't know.

You then move to the Support Box. This is the phase in which you're supporting the person to fine-tune the task. You just encourage him or her to keep up the good work, great job, or suggest minor changes. You, as the mentor, are essentially there for moral support. This phase is called "conscious competence." You know what you know.

Finally, you move to the last phase, which is simply to just do it. The true delegation box. You know when you've reached this phase: it's when you can say three words and the person gets what you mean and can complete the task. This phase is called "unconscious competence"; you can do it without thinking about it.

This is a very powerful tool that I've used with my clients and shared with my students. I've told people to keep this chart at their desks to remind themselves of the art of delegation. The response I get from most executives who want to improve their delegation skills is that they don't have time to do all these phases. I tell them they do, especially since there's always time to redo the task completely. When things go wrong in delegation, it's pretty easy to pinpoint whether you've skipped one or all these phases. When you go right to delegate and skip all the other phases of mentoring, you'll find yourself saying I should just do it myself, it's so much easier than trying to explain it. If you find yourself doing that, you're either surrounding yourself with the wrong people or you're not delegating effectively, and ultimately you're not mentoring your staff to grow.

Whether you're doing the delegating or being delegated to, you have equal responsibility to understand the process. If you're being delegated to and don't think you completely understand the assignment, then it's your responsibility to ask the person delegating to reexplain the task. If you still don't understand the task, keep

PEOPLE = 6

BALLS = 5

FIGURE 5
The tennis ball exercise
demonstrates the equal
importance of how
information is both received
and delivered.

asking questions until you're confident you can complete the task. If you're the person delegating, it's your responsibility to make certain that that person understands your directions. We all know that moment when we think someone's heard us, but in our head we're saying, "OK, that's good enough"—we also know there's a good chance the outcome won't be what we want it to be. You should keep explaining if you feel this way, because good enough is never enough. If you think they only heard part of it and think they can move it forward, you might want them to take the task to a certain point and report back to you before they complete the task. This way you can adjust the outcome quickly if they're on the wrong path.

To help firms learn the skills of mentoring, I often hold company retreats to work on management skills and also set goals for the coming year. One exercise in teamwork I do at a company retreat is to put the group in a circle. At one particular retreat, there were eight people in the circle, and I slowly handed tennis balls to one person to start throwing around the circle. If N equals the number of people in the circle, then the most balls you can have in motion is N minus 1. Why? Because it's almost impossible to throw and catch at the same time. The purpose of the exercise is to demonstrate the importance of an individual's action. People are much more concerned about catching the ball than throwing it. What this demonstrates is that it's equally important to the success of the exercise that the person you're throwing to catches the ball as that you are able to catch the ball. If you're less concerned about how you deliver information than with how you receive it, you'll ultimately fail at delegation. You have to be equally adept at both.

FIGURE 5

While delegating is only one piece of the puzzle of mentoring and growing your staff, the frequency of how often you're mentoring your staff is equally significant. You want people to be in a growing environment all the time. The challenge many firms face today is a restless talent pool of people who want to grow faster than their skills grow. No matter how educated someone is, there's no substitute for experience. What you learn from being involved in a project, no matter what phase it's in, is very different from what's taught in school. Nothing is better than the hands-on knowledge of having the experience. You need to have these experiences to grasp the design profession. You need to make mistakes and grow from those mistakes.

An example of an effective and established mentoring program is the AIA's Intern Development Program (IDP). Its purpose is to establish elements of training that are important to the architectural practice. Before a person can be licensed, he or she must go through an IDP program with a firm. The intern identifies a mentor to supervise him or her through the program and trains under the direction of that registered architect.

Several areas of expertise are addressed. They include design and construction documents, construction-contract administration, management, and professional community services. Time is allocated as follows: design and construction documentation, 2,800 hours; construction-contract management, 560 hours; management, 280 hours; and professional community services, 80 hours. You're also required to have an additional 1,880 hours in elective training in any of the above categories. This brings the total of hours required to complete the IDP to 5,600.*

Internships are an essential part of understanding the profession in a whole new light when you're in school. If it weren't for my internship at Gensler, I don't think I could've found my path in this profession to know what I would've been most suited for in my career. I might still be struggling as an architect had I not seen early on that I needed to find a niche where the practice needed me and I needed it.

Mentoring can come in all forms and shapes, and like delegation it's important that both parties are completely engaged in the process. If you want to grow, you must always be willing to learn.

What employees want is to be stretched beyond their day-to-day tasks. No matter how inexperienced people are, they need to be challenged to grow. Finding small ways to test their skills and

To learn more about IDP in architecture, see http://www.ncarb.org/Experience-Through-Internships/~/media/Files/PDF/Guidelines/idp_guidelines.ashx.

expand their experiences helps people grow. In some companies there are slack-time lists that allow for people to take on different tasks outside their everyday work when things are slow or they're waiting for direction. These tasks are important but not urgent. It might be to build on a detail library or research work, all things that you'd love to accomplish if only you had the time. This way you can keep your staff productive when there are lulls in the schedule. Anybody can add to the slack-time list; it simply needs to be approved by someone in authority to make sure the tasks are worth performing.

Another way to grow your staff is to promote the idea of information flowing from the bottom up. Art Gensler used to ask me why I thought all the information had to come from the top down. It would be refreshing if ideas were also generated by the people on the frontlines. I was one of those people who looked at things considered "sacred cows" in the office, tasks that everyone did without question just because they had always been done that way. I would ask why do it this way when it might be more efficient another way. I always took a proactive approach to improve the organizations where I worked, and in my own company I encourage people to do the same. Some of the best ideas don't come from the principals of the companies we work with but from their staff. Encouraging people to speak up builds an environment of growth and learning.

EMPLOYEE BENEFITS

Another indication of how well a firm treats its employees is directly related to the benefit package offered to employees. Keep in mind that the greater the financial health of the firm, the more benefits it should be able to offer. The following are the typical benefits I have seen offered in design firms.

HEALTH INSURANCE

Most firms offer health benefits to their employees. Most of the time the basic coverage is offered, and if an employee chooses to upgrade the plan, then he or she pays for the difference in cost. In addition, if an employee has a spouse and a family, he or she typically pays for the additional costs for the family members. In some cases firms offer this benefit to their management.

TIME OFF

The most common time-off benefits are:

1. Vacation time: two weeks for the first five years of employment, three weeks for employees who have been with the firm for five years, and four weeks for employees who have been with the firm for ten or more years
2. Sick time: five days per year
3. Holidays: the average is seven paid holidays per year.
4. Paid time off (PTO): some firms combine all of the days off and provide what they call PTO time.
5. Most firms require people to earn their time off by accruing a certain amount of hours each month.

EDUCATION ALLOWANCES

Many firms create an education allowance for their employees. This usually requires an employee to submit a request for educational dollars to be paid for by the firm if the classes are relevant to the employee's position.

BONUS PROGRAMS

Many firms provide for a bonus program to compensate employees for efforts above and beyond their day-to-day responsibilities.

PROFIT-SHARING PROGRAMS

Many firms offer 401(k) plans that allow for retirement savings. These funds can come either directly from the employee's salary or from the firm's profits being distributed each year.

HIRING PRACTICES

When it comes time to grow your company, it's important to evaluate the skill sets of your current staff. It's always better when possible to promote from within than to search outside your firm for talent.

When hiring from within, the message you want to send to your staff is that you've created a place of growth and advancement. It's important for them to know that they can advance within your company, provided they can gain the experience required for the role they want to grow into. Many people like to have job descriptions in their employee manuals, and the effective ones are the ones people use to know what's expected of them to advance. It provides a road map for advancement to know what the requirements are for people to grow to the next level.

If the talent doesn't exist in your organization, you have no choice but to reach outside your company to find the right people. It'll be important to explain to your staff why you must go outside the firm to hire for this position. Smart people understand this, and they also understand that their growth will benefit from having access to other smart experienced people.

When you hire from outside you'll need to follow the steps mentioned earlier in this chapter in the section "Finding the Right Fit." Again, it's more important to hire first for fit and second for skill.

FIRM STRUCTURE

How should your firm be structured to create the most efficient organization? If you have an organization that doesn't have layers of reporting, or for that matter much structure, you'll be challenged with two major issues. First, the distance between you as the principal and the junior person reporting to you is too great and puts a greater burden on your delegation skills. Second, you'll run into the problem that too many people are reporting directly to you. The rule of thumb is that one person can be responsible for no more than ten people at a time. If you want to grow your firm, you'll need to learn how to leverage your talents to others to manage more staff. A full explanation of the different structures found in a design practice can be found in chapter 5, "Project Management."

Job descriptions are important for structure, but people seem to find them puzzling. Some people love them; some people deplore them. But job descriptions are a necessary evil. Why? Because they help people understand what's expected of them in their position and if they want to grow into the next position. The problem with job descriptions is that it's difficult to define all that you need someone to do in a written document. People who don't like them don't like them because they think their employees will say, "That's not in my job description." If you ever hear those words, those should be the last words you hear from that employee. You don't need people in your organization who are looking at a piece of paper to tell them what to do.

The other issue with job descriptions and titles is that the same word means different things in different companies, and a different title can mean the same thing in a different company. A project manager in one firm can be the equivalent of a job captain in another firm. Smaller firms often give less experienced people the chance to grow faster, because there's less layering in the organization. If an individual joins a large firm, he or she may get to work on larger-scale projects, but his or her responsibilities will be less broad and he or she may not grow as fast. In smaller firms an employee may be stretched to enhance his or her skills, but the projects may not offer as much challenge. There are pros and cons to working in larger versus smaller firms, but the important thing to take into account is whether the individual is in a firm that allows for learning and growth.

Here's a list of titles that you may come across in the design world. Job descriptions for the project-related titles are in chapter 5, "Project Management."

Project titles (associated with running projects): partner, principal, design director, senior project designer, senior project manager, senior designer, project manager, job captain, project architect, draftsperson, expeditor, CAD operator, junior designer, junior draftsperson, intern (you can add landscape, interior, or engineer to the front of any of these titles for those disciplines).

Office titles (associated with running the firm): partner, principal, chief executive officer, chief financial officer, chief operating officer, director of marketing, director of finance and administration, CAD manager, studio director, studio manager, marketing coordinator, bookkeeper, accounting clerk, office manager, executive assistant, administrative assistant, receptionist, office assistant.

Promotional titles (titles given to people solely for the purpose of being promoted for their contribution to the betterment of the firm and not for any specific role change): partner, associate partner, principal, vice president, senior associate, associate.

Let me share some thoughts about using promotional titles. Some firms have very loose criteria as to what it takes to become, say, an associate of the firm. Some base it solely on longevity; others on level of responsibilities. I believe a title should be awarded to employees for showing dedication to the firm in multiple ways. They should be looking out for the betterment of the firm and not just themselves or their projects; they should be able to promote the firm's culture internally and to the outside world. They should be performing tasks necessary to operating the firm but still outside their day-to-day responsibilities. You must consider whether the promotion will send the right message to the staff about who you are as a firm and what you expect from your leaders. If the message falls short, then you should seriously reconsider promoting someone.

When it comes time to consider people for promotion to partner or principal, they must have an indispensible value to your firm. Not necessarily irreplaceable (you can say that on some level, everyone is replaceable), but the firm would be at a loss without these people on board. Picking who you want as a partner is a serious decision that can be equated to marriage. It's a relationship that you don't enter into lightly, and you want to make certain it'll be around for a long time. The most significant role a partner brings to the table is the ability to bring in work and attract clients. In some cities, such as New York, you cannot be a partner in an architectural firm without being a registered architect. This eliminates many people who have all the qualifications but not a license. In other states, like California, you can be a corporation with partners, and those partners don't need to be licensed to be owners in the company.

Specific questions to ask yourself when considering a partner:

1. Is this a partner that adds value to your company?
2. Does this person fit within the culture of your company?
3. Is this the person that if something should happen to you can carry on the firm?
4. Does this person have an indispensible quality?
5. How long has this person been with your company? If less than two years, I'd question whether that's long enough to be able to evaluate this promotion.
6. Does your staff look up to this person as a leader?
7. Are clients comfortable with this person?
8. Is the design quality or their unique talent at or above par with the work being produced by the firm?
9. Are you 100 percent certain this person is committed to your firm?

OWNERSHIP TRANSITION

Once you ask yourself these questions, and if you can answer them in a positive way, the next step is to start an ownership transition plan.

Ownership in your company should never be given away—ownership encourages accountability. It's akin to a rent-a-car: when's the last time you washed one? If it's not yours, you tend not to take care of it in the same way. If people realize that their hard-earned dollars are going into buying the company, they'll treat that investment very differently than if they're simply receiving a bonus for their shares of ownership.

The process of ownership transition is a book in itself. I won't try to abridge the information here, but I do recommend that you search for books on ownership transition in design firms: they do exist.* That being said, here's an outline of the steps to help you understand the process of ownership transition.

1 **UNDERSTAND WHAT YOUR OBJECTIVES** are for creating an ownership-transition program. Are you selling shares because you want partners or need partners, or because the people you're doing this for have earned the right to obtain ownership in your company? The shift from being a sole proprietor to a partner is not always the easiest. In the past you could make all the decisions on your own, and you could spend the company funds any way you chose. When you bring in partners you have an obligation to create transparency in your business and to allow them to know exactly how the company is performing both functionally and financially. When you make choices about clients, employees, and financial matters, you'll have to consult with your partners. Whether they're a 2 percent owner or a 50 percent owner, if you want them to be true partners, then you'll want to engage them in these decisions. Like any change in a company, it takes time to settle in and to understand the relationships you've created. Some are seamless and some take work.

2 **IDENTIFY YOUR CANDIDATES.** Make certain you conduct your due diligence to really determine the right candidates for ownership in your company. It's my recommendation that this person never be brought in from the outside and immediately made an owner, no matter how much expertise he or she possesses. If you're merging your firm with someone else, then you won't have a choice, but if you're selling shares of stock or a piece of your partnership, you'll want to make sure this is the right person.

3 **VALUE YOUR COMPANY.** There will be a need to assess the value of your company to determine what it's worth and how

*Visit www.thebusiness ofdesign.net for suggestions.

130

much each person will be paying to become an owner. Whether it's based on sales or profits or a combination of the two, the value of your company should be discounted for internal buy-ins (versus an external purchase). That is, if you're selling shares of your company to people who helped create the current value, you might want to discount the cost of his or her shares in proportion to their overall contribution. In other words, someone who's increased the value significantly by his or her contribution to the firm would receive a greater discount than someone with a lesser contribution. It's also important to explain to future owners that although some people might have made a large contribution to the success of your company before you considered them for partnership, they must understand that you were taking all the risk during that time and they held none of that burden. The reason that an outside purchase is typically higher is that you're giving up more control when you're selling to a third party versus selling to one of your employees. At times the determined value for a third party can be as much as double the selling price to an employee, but that's based on many factors.

④ DO I SELL MY COMPANY to my future partners or give them a bonus to pay for the company?

⑤ PRESENTING A TERM SHEET to your candidate. Once you've established your firm's value, you'll then present that value to the candidate, along with a term sheet to spell out all the other terms associated with the purchase. These include the number of shares you're selling or what percentage of the company you're offering, who's selling the stock or shares (typically the current owners sell their shares to the individuals, but the company can issue new shares if it chooses to take that direction), payment of shares (this is how the candidate will pay for the shares), restrictions on the shares (how they can be disposed), a list of documents to be signed, and a timeline for the process.

⑥ REPRESENTATION FOR YOUR CANDIDATE. The candidate should have different representation than your firm's attorney. Some firms offer to pay for these costs as part of the transition benefits. I recommend that you establish a budget to pay for these expenses.

⑦ DOCUMENTS TO BE SIGNED. There will be many documents to be signed to complete this transaction. These include the following: stock purchase agreement (this is for corporations selling stock); promissory note (if you're going to finance the sale for your employee); stock pledge agreement (this pledges the stock for financing the shares); shareholder agreement (this is the main document that details all the conditions of the ownership); shareholder indemnification agreement (this indemnifies the parties from each other for selling shares in the company).

BUILDING A LEGACY FIRM

There is always the question of whether designers can actually build a legacy firm—a firm that lives beyond its founders. There are plenty of good examples in the commercial design firm arena, such as Skidmore, Owings & Merrill (SOM) or Helmuth Obata and Kassabaum (HOK). But this case is rare with more boutique firms. Most designers have attached their names to the firm's name. Once that person retires or dies, usually the firm does the same. One good example of a legacy firm that has continued on after the owner was tragically killed is the interior design firm of Jed Johnson. Jed died aboard TWA flight 800 over Long Island on July 17, 1996. The firm was taken over by Jed's twin brother, Jay, who allowed the talents of the firm to be placed in the capable hands of Arthur Dunham and others, and through the skill of their practice and the relationships they've built, the firm lives on.

If it's your desire to build a firm that continues on after you, then you'll need to think about who'll be adept at carrying on the practice. You should also consider that you might need to add these people's names to your firm name to allow for public recognition. One mistake that many principals make is to look to their peers as successors when in fact they should be looking to the next generation. There's little use in trying to build a legacy firm by selecting people who are all the same age.

Many firms transition from a single name to a group of names or an acronym of those names. This can be helpful because it lowers

FIGURE 6 The author facilitating a retreat in Palm Springs with a client in the Elrod House designed by the architect John Lautner. Having inspiring venues to hold retreats enhances your ability to expand your goals and perspective.

the expectation of clients that they're going to get only the name on the door. Of course, in high-profile projects the expectation is that you *will* get the name on the door to work on your project.

The transitioning of a firm is never without challenges. At the end of the process the most significant issue is whether the founding members' wishes for continuity are met.

CORPORATE RETREATS

I facilitate annual retreats for many of the firms we work with, and the ones that consistently have these retreats year after year grow faster. Companies willing to get off their daily treadmill and take a look at themselves are the ones that find new ways to run their businesses. These are management retreats focused on improving the firm's management and helping the leaders understand how they want their firms to grow. What we like to incorporate are learning techniques that allow people to step out of their comfort zones to learn something new and experience a new way to think.

FIGURE 6

The following are some questions I'm always asked about our retreats:

1 **WHO SHOULD ATTEND THE RETREAT?** The answer to this question is simple. The people who should attend are the people most likely to contribute to the growth of your firm, not for their role in projects but for their role in the overall contribution to the organization's health.

2 **WHAT'S THE BEST SIZE FOR AN EFFECTIVE RETREAT? SHOULD IT INCLUDE THE ENTIRE OFFICE?** If the number of participants becomes larger than twelve, the retreat's effectiveness is compromised. You want everyone to be involved and to contribute, and once you increase the size beyond twelve there's little room for individual contribution. We also tend to have people who don't participate when the group is too large. I've conducted retreats that are a hybrid between management and staff. These retreats bring the management team in first, to work on specific tasks, and then bring the next tier into the retreat for a one-day session. This allows you see the level of engagement you receive from the next tier of staff and to identify your rising stars. It also allows for buy-in from your employees to get them on board with the coming changes of the organization, because they'll feel like they've been a part of authoring the changes.

3 **HOW LONG SHOULD A TYPICAL RETREAT BE?** We recommend that retreats be a minimum of two days, with a social event midway. The reason for this is best illustrated by a story about the first retreat that I ever facilitated. The company's founding partner had recently passed away, and I was brought in to help facilitate a plan for the firm's future and its potential for growth and reorganization. What I identified early on was that the dynamic of the five remaining principals was very different principal to principal. In some cases they were willing to collaborate, but in other cases they were out-and-out competitors, even though they were partners. The past owner had purposely put each of them in a competitive role, thinking that it would be a motivator to build a diverse practice. It did the complete opposite and put them at odds with each other.

A legal document was drawn up that created a stipulation that upon the death of the previous owner each new owner had to stay for three years before his or her ownership accrued fully. To deal with the tension, the principals decided to hire someone to help them change the firm's dynamic. At this first retreat—which despite my recommendation was only a single day—we needed to address the issues that existed between the partners and then take those issues and build on them to mend the firm. There was so much tearing down of the dynamics of the old regime, there wasn't enough time to plan a restructuring strategy to strengthen their partnership. By the time dinner came around, no one wanted to eat with each other and everyone simply went home angry.

The lesson this taught me was that all retreats need to be a minimum of two days. Day one to tear down the issues. Evening one to break bread and realize that this is just business, but we do actually enjoy each other's company. And day two to build back what was torn down the previous day. For nineteen years I haven't deviated from this formula, and it works. I've added to the number of days when the issues were broad, but only when needed.

❹ WHY HAVE A RETREAT? It's what I call "the treadmill theory." If you're on a treadmill every day, leaving the office is like getting off the treadmill and taking a run outdoors. You need to get out of your environment and into one where you are freed from distractions. You need to find a place that's relaxing yet productive. If you work in the city, then go to the country. Locations that are about two hours away from your office are perfect, because people feel they're getting away without having to spend a lot of time traveling. People will stay focused when you narrow the issues around your retreat agenda and nothing else. When people are in a new environment with their coworkers, they tend to be sharing the same experiences with each other, and it becomes a bonding time to help build their relationship. It can take place in resort towns, islands, mountains, deserts, or cities. The most successful places are the ones where people are all having the same experience at the same time.

⑤ WHAT ELSE DO YOU DO ON RETREATS THAT IS OF INTEREST TO THE PARTICIPANTS? Often when I first recommend a retreat to a new client, the first question is: "This is not some kind of touchy-feely thing, is it?" My answer is always the same, no walking on hot rocks or climbing telephone poles, although I think there are lessons to be learned from that kind of retreat. During the retreats it's beneficial if you can incorporate a side trip to a completed project or a significant architectural location. One year we had a retreat in the Elrod house (1968) designed by John Lautner. It was simply an inspiration to be in the house during the retreat, and it also was fun because it was featured in the James Bond movie *Diamonds Are Forever* (1971).

⑥ WHAT DO YOU DO TO MAKE SURE THAT THE WORK COMPLETED ON THE RETREAT CONTINUES TO MOVE FORWARD? During the retreat we're always keeping a to-do list, which is tallied at the end. This list is then vetted to make certain it represents the most important goals for the coming year. Each to-do is assigned to a single person—never more than one person, because when two people are assigned a task, it rarely gets done. Assigning one person doesn't mean that person needs to complete the task, he or she just needs to be responsible for its progress and will be held accountable for its completion. Each task is assigned a deadline for completion. Once a quarter we review the tasks to make certain progress is being made and those assigned are being held accountable for the task. The truth is, no one wants to return to the next retreat being the person who didn't complete the task. If it becomes apparent that the wrong person is assigned to a task or if the task is deemed unachievable, then it can be reassigned or simply taken off the list.

Just for fun I want to share my worst retreat experience. I have probably facilitated a couple of hundred retreats over the years. I once had a client who was very democratic in his thinking and wanted to include his entire staff on the firm's first retreat. I reluctantly agreed and allowed the whole office to attend. The first day was productive, but quite a few junior staff members didn't participate. After the sessions were completed, we all went out for a social dinner. That night after dinner we all went to bed to get ready for an early morning start time. So we thought. It turned out that two of the management team members decided to host a cocktail party in their room. The next morning three people were missing (one being a senior member of the management team), and six other people showed up physically but mentally were anything but present. That was the last retreat of the entire staff for that firm. Retreats are expensive and time-consuming, and you truly want to get the most you can from the event. My last book will be a tell-all about the one hundred-plus retreats I've facilitated. But as I said, it'll be my *last* book.

> "All your dreams can come true if you have the courage to pursue them." —*WALT DISNEY*

Victoria Hagan

KG: What are some of the greatest challenges that are presented to you in running your own business?

VH: I think in running your own business there are always many, many challenges. It's a constant juggling act. The goal at the end of the day for me is to do good work and have happy clients. It's also managing my team, keeping them motivated and working seamlessly together. It's troubleshooting issue after issue. I think the interior design business is just full of small day-to-day problems, and it's probably not the right field for someone who is not inherently a problem solver.

KG: Do you enjoy the juggling part of it?

VH: I love working with people. I love collaborating with architects, designers, and tradespeople in developing a project. The creative process is always better when challenged.

KG: What percentage do you think of the process is creative, and how much is problem solving?

VH: I would say a quarter of it is the creative process.

KG: How would you think the design profession has changed since you started?

VH: The industry as a whole has become more professional. A lot is expected of me, and I expect a lot of others. Technology has totally transformed the way we operate. Everything's digital—it's quicker. It's much quicker, and it's much more visual.

KG: I would agree that it's much easier to show clients a visual image that can help them understand what you are thinking rather than showing them just a fabric sample or a picture of a chair.

VH: Absolutely. And you know, all our drawings are computerized on CAD. It's funny, I still sketch over the computerized drawings, but I do think it makes it all more efficient.

KG: How would you describe the perfect client?

VH: Trusting. And with a sense of humor, because the process should be fun. I think the perfect client is looking for something that makes you a better designer. The perfect client challenges you to be better than who you think you are. I feel very fortunate because I've had really very special clients, and I have grown as a designer because of working with them.

KG: Do you feel that the perfect client also is knowledgeable about the process?

VH: Not necessarily. I don't think they need to have done this before, but having a vision of how they want to live is helpful, and that comes from an understanding of themselves. My job is to capture that lifestyle in their homes.

KG: You have branched out into product development. What inspired you to take that route?

VH: I had always wanted to design products and fabric, and I found myself at a place in my career when I couldn't find certain pieces of furniture or certain kinds of textiles. As an interior designer, I know what is needed. I think I understand what makes a good coffee table. I know what makes a comfortable chair. I think I have an interesting perspective, and I certainly have my own point of view, which is, I like to say, classic American. My designs mix well with both period and more contemporary pieces. Again, it's ultimately about the vision. Being an interior designer and designing furniture and fabric is something I always wanted to do. Once I was able to articulate my vision, it all came about very organically.

KG: Speaking of your career, who inspired you?
VH: My mother early on—she was very creative—and my father, who always had high expectations. My years at Parsons were a real turning point for me. I can't say enough about the importance of a good design education. You know I always look back to my internship with Simone Feldman, who later became my partner. She was my mentor, and she had many more years of experience than I, and I guess I had the drive. I learned so much from her in the short time we were in business together. Unfortunately, she passed away in 1991, but she inspired me a great deal.

KG: How do you want to be remembered?
VH: How do I want to be remembered? First and foremost as a great mother and a kind person, and ultimately I think that helps shape me as a designer. I'd like to think that I brought a unique perspective to the world of interior design that made for beautiful homes and happy clients.

CHAPTER 5

Project Management

I once heard someone say that mastery of the rules leads to limitless expression, and this struck me as appropriate to any creative profession. No matter what business you're in, understanding the rules of the game allows you to take liberties with them and to express your process in a way that works well for you.

For a design firm, project management is what sets the successful firms apart from the struggling ones. If you can master how a project is managed, it can influence so many other parts of your organization. When projects are successful, you'll have happy clients, happy employees, happy consultants, and ultimately a very happy place for you to work.

PROJECT VISION STATEMENT
———————————————————

CLIENT: MR. DAVID BEACH

NAME OF PROJECT: UPPER WEST SIDE BROWNSTONE

DATE: JANUARY 2011

PROJECT DESCRIPTION: STANDARD SIX, APARTMENT RENOVATION

VISION STATEMENT:

"To Create a Home That Can Evolve as Their Growing Family Evolves"

FIGURE 1
Sample project vision
statement, which should be
developed at the beginning
of a project

PROJECT KICKOFF

A successful project management system all starts when a project is first launched. If you jump right in without any forethought, you jeopardize the project's outcome. Having a method to allow a project to get off on the right foot will set the tone for the entire project, and determining some facts at the onset will help guide the team members as they move through the project and will aid any new team members as they enter the project along the way.

❶ VISION Create a vision for your project, understanding that this should be a combination of your vision as a firm as well as the vision the client has expressed for the project. FIGURE 1

Years ago I was consulting for an architect who was having difficulty engaging his clients, a couple, in the project. The clients were going through the motions of building a house without seeming to have a purpose. When I asked the architect if there was anything unusual about this family, it came out that they had recently lost a child. They wanted a new home, not to forget their son but to move their life into a place that was not so burdened with death. They thought a new home would help usher in a new phase of their life. Not only was this family building a new home, they were rebuilding their lives.

I suggested that they treat this project as a healing process, to help them move through this difficult phase. Healing became the vision for this project, and I told the architect to ask subtle questions to engage the owners in the process and to understand this vision. Building a home is a very personal thing, and it takes a little bit of design, a little bit of talent, and a whole lot of psychology to get through it. My client asked questions such as "How do you want to honor your son?" and "What was special about your old house that you want us to bring to this new home?" The process greatly improved. In the end everyone was extremely satisfied with the project.

I bring this up to point out that the vision for your home, office, hospital, or institution may not always be about the architecture;

143

it may be about an experience or a need that you should try to identify. I tell my clients all the time who are residential architects: a house is a product, a home is a process. You need to go through the process to create a home.

② **BUDGET** As much as possible, you need to know the project budget. Be careful of clients who tell you that there's no budget. There's always a budget.

> **Designer:** What's your budget?
>
> **Client:** We have no budget.
>
> **Designer:** If we do this, we believe it'll be right for you, and we'll probably spend $5 million.
>
> **Client:** I don't want to spend any more than $3 million.

Voilà, you have a budget. Of course, the next step is to figure out if you can complete the project within the client's budget.

③ **THE DECISION MAKER** You need to know immediately who the decision maker is on the project. You can waste hundreds of hours going down the wrong path if you're listening to the wrong person. I always tell my residential clients that if two parties are involved in the project, they must be at every meeting. The person spending the money is as important as the person writing the check.

④ **TEAM** Again, as much as possible you need to identify the team both internally and externally. It's also vitally important to the project's success to identify each team member's role.

⑤ **SCHEDULE** Determine a preliminary schedule for the project that can be continually updated. The more you can match your performance with client expectations, the better the project process will be. FIGURE 2

⑥ **EXPECTATIONS** You should document client and firm expectations from the beginning. These will most likely shift during the process, but it's healthy to see at the project's end whether you met the client's and your own expectations, and it's an opportunity to see how those expectations changed throughout the project. Expectations might be design related, but they can also deal with performance, vision, budget, and a number of points raised at the project's start.

Once you've established the team, schedule, and budget, it's time to start designing the project. Project management has the potential to be many books in itself.* This chapter offers an overview of the subject, focusing on team structure, roles, project monitoring, and reporting.

Adelphi Research Lab   Retrieve Mode: All Data * ETC/JTD Date: 5/31/2008

Labor | Consultant | Expense | General | Rates | Top-down Plan | Analysis

Labor   New Row   Delete   Insert   Employee   Generic   Search   Indent   Outdent   Shift

Description	Project	Start	Finish	Planned Hrs	Subrow	2005 3/3 - 12/31	2006 1/1 - 12/31	2007 1/1 - 12/31	Q1 2008 Jan 2008	Q1 2008 Feb 2008	Q1 2008 Mar 2008	Q2 2008 Apr 2008	Q2 2008 May 2008	Q2 200 Jun 200
⊟ Adelphi Research Lab	2003005.00	4/5/2005	12/1/2108	12,850	Gantt									
					Baseline Hrs									
					Revenue	155,267	374,240	503,520	8,512	9,344	14,272	16,128	28,992	8,0(
⊞ PreDesign	2003005.00	4/5/2005	, 8/20/2010	7,577	Gantt									
					Baseline Hrs									
					Revenue	77,193	271,712	374,288	8,512	8,064	8,128	8,448	8,512	8,0(
⊞ Schematic Design	2003005.00	4/25/2005	11/30/2007	2,272	Gantt									
					Baseline Hrs									
					Revenue	78,074	102,528	112,160						
⊞ Design Development	2003005.00	3/3/2007	12/1/2108	661	Gantt									
					Baseline Hrs									
					Revenue		16,368							
⊞ Construction Documents	2003005.00	5/2/2007	11/23/2009	1,319	Gantt									
					Baseline Hrs									
					Revenue			704						
⊞ Bidding Negotiation	2003005.00	2/1/2008	11/22/2009	634	Gantt									
					Baseline Hrs									
					Revenue					1,280	6,144	7,680	20,480	
⊞ Construction Administration	2003005.00	4/24/2009	11/15/2009	387	Gantt									
					Baseline Hrs									
					Revenue									

FIGURE 2
Sample project delivery
timeline

*For a list of suggested books, visit www. thebusinessofdesign.net

TEAM STRUCTURE AND ROLES

Most of my clients know that I'm a big proponent of the studio system as a way to structure the organization. The studio system breaks the office into smaller pods—teams—that work closely together. Small offices may have one or two studios, and larger ones, many more. Some studios are divided by expertise, others by discipline, and some merely by size. As I mentioned in the previous chapter, people are capable of managing effectively when there are no more than ten people reporting directly to one manager.

Some firms divide studios up by discipline such as landscape, interiors, or architecture. Other firms divide up by expertise. These studios might be design, production, or construction. My personal preference is to divide studios by discipline. This allows employees to gain a more well-rounded professional experience and not be pigeonholed. You want to create an environment of collaboration and integration.

The following charts outline the different structures we see in design practices. FIGURES 3–5

STUDIO STRUCTURE BY DISCIPLINE

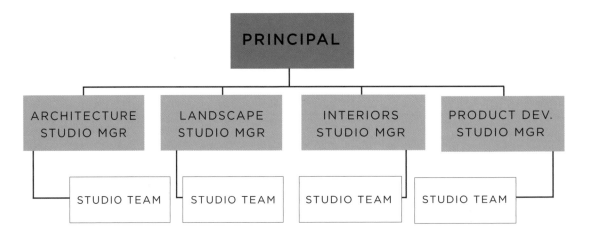

STUDIO STRUCTURE BY EXPERTISE

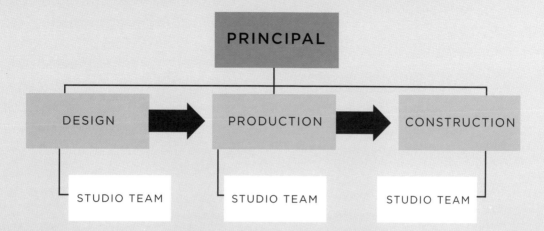

LESS STRUCTURED ARCHITECTURAL PRACTICE

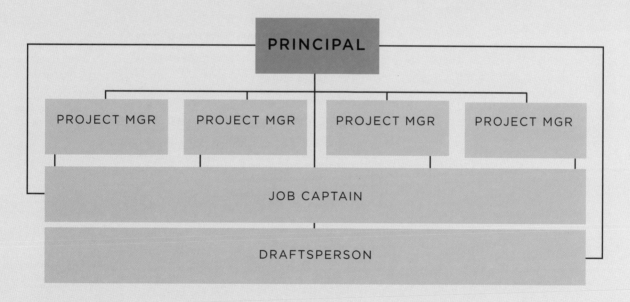

FIGURE 3 Organizational chart showing a design
firm structured by discipline

FIGURE 4 Organizational chart showing a design
firm structured by expertise

FIGURE 5 Organizational chart showing a design
firm with little or no structure

The following is a list of titles typically found in architectural firms and in interior design firms, accompanied by a description of the position.

ARCHITECTURE

PRINCIPAL/PARTNER-IN-CHARGE: The principal has the overall responsibility for achieving the firm's goals and growth plans and has ultimate responsibility for employee and client satisfaction.

Specific responsibilities can include:

- Cultivating and securing new business
- Managing the firm's direction
- Developing and promoting the firm's vision, mission, core values, and long-range plans
- Structuring the organization to ensure maximum efficiency, employee satisfaction, and growth
- Participating in creating and positioning the firm to take advantage of opportunities for growth and marketplace expansion
- Assuming the leadership role of operational functions necessary to run the firm, including, but not limited to, human resources, marketing, financial administration, and quality enhancement and professional growth for the firm

PROJECT MANAGER: The project manager acts as the leader of the project team to manage the development and delivery of various projects under the supervision of the principal-in–charge. The project manager is the primary client contact for the project and acts as the project implementer, responsible for creating and distributing all necessary information to all the members involved in executing the vision.

Specific responsibilities can include:

- Prioritizing, delegating, and coordinating work assignments and project team members' tasks

- Coordinating job site visits and agendas as directed by project leaders
- Managing financial and administrative aspects of projects, including implementing schedules, preparing and coordinating cost estimate budgets, and overseeing maintenance of necessary logs and records to manage project
- Overseeing construction, including preparing contractor documents and creating punch lists

JOB CAPTAIN: The job captain supports the development and delivery of numerous simultaneous projects under the direction of the project manager. The job captain assists with prioritizing, delegating, and coordinating project tasks among support staff and consultants for the each project.

Specific responsibilities can include:
- Maintaining logs and records necessary to manage the projects
- Processing construction documents through plan check
- Composing transmittals, preparing site analysis documents and other correspondence as necessary
- Coordinating presentation work, including materials and color palettes

PROJECT ARCHITECT: The project architect assists with the development and delivery of an individual project from inception to construction.

Specific responsibilities can include:
- Performance drafting, including creating or delegating the development of conceptual sketches
- Performing or delegating presentation work for the project, as well as design development of the project
- Developing conceptual sketches into design presentation and developing sketch details into construction documents

- Scheduling, budgeting, and overseeing work assignments of project staff with project manager and job captain

DRAFTSPERSON: The draftsperson assists with the design and documentation of the drawings for a specific project.

Specific responsibilities can include:
- Drawing and preparing contract documents under the direction of job captain
- Researching codes and city ordinances

INTERN: The intern provides assistance to all staff, from design staff to business administration. This is an entry-level position and specific responsibilities can vary greatly.

Specific responsibilities can include:
- Assisting designers with project management and preparing presentation material for client meetings
- Assisting with general office administration, including providing copies and filing, maintaining office equipment and office supplies, maintaining sample and resource libraries, and running errands, including pickups and deliveries
- Preparing office mailings, receiving deliveries, and answering phones

INTERIOR DESIGN

PRINCIPAL/PARTNER-IN-CHARGE: The description is the same as under "Architecture" above.

SENIOR DESIGNER: The senior designer acts as leader to the project team and manages the design development of specific projects. The senior designer plans and executes the presentation of these designs in graphic forms or in detailed scale models.

Specific responsibilities can include:

- Liaising with principal, clients, contractors, consultants, vendors, and employees
- Overseeing the design for a client and ensuring that the designs fit with the client's expectations
- Selecting all furnishings for approval by the principal-in-charge
- Maintaining the project's overall design direction and aesthetic
- Managing the delivery of the project
- Managing and mentoring design staff
- Overseeing installation

DESIGNER: The designer supports the development and delivery of various projects under the supervision of the senior designer.

Specific responsibilities can include:

- Performing computer and manual drafting for various projects, including developing sketch details into CAD or manual drawings
- Assisting in the selection of furnishings, including furniture, textiles, flooring, paint and stain finishes, accessories, and lighting
- Assisting expeditor or design assistant in the expediting of purchasing for a specific project
- Developing conceptual sketches into design presentations
- Preparing construction documents
- Maintaining logs and records, and composing documentation and correspondence necessary for the project

DESIGN ASSISTANT: The design assistant provides assistance to all design staff and business staff. The design assistant is an entry-level position.

Specific responsibilities can include:

- Assisting designers with project management and decorative aspects of projects
- Researching and shopping for fabrics, furniture, lighting, wall

coverings, antiques, carpeting, and accessories as requested by designers

- Sourcing online resources for projects and interacting with vendors for quotes and order questions
- Helping prepare presentation material for client meetings
- Creating and maintaining tracking grids for status reporting, project schedules, and client binders

EXPEDITOR: The expeditor assists the design team by coordinating with the design team all furnishings to be purchased through the firm.

Primary responsibilities can include:
- Purchasing all furnishings and materials specified by the design team for the project
- Creating proposals and purchase orders
- Creating contingency plans for delays associated with the final installation

Other less project-specific roles for both interior design and architectural firms include the following roles.

DESIGN DIRECTOR: The design director oversees the design for a client and liaises with the client and senior project designer to ensure that the designs match with the client's expectations and the company's identity. The design director also manages the conceptualization, design, and construction of new products.

Primary responsibilities can include:
- Overseeing and ensuring the general direction of the firm's design vision
- Serving as liaison and primary point of contact between the principals and designers
- Overseeing the approval of design direction and visioning for each project as it's conceived

- Researching and establishing relationships with new vendors to enhance the overall design aesthetic of the firm

DIRECTOR OF PRODUCTION: The director of production works closely with project managers and staff to ensure that the standard of production is being upheld throughout the firm.

> Specific responsibilities can include:

- Managing and scheduling the entire production system for all projects in the office
- Researching new technology for the betterment of the firm and its production capabilities
- Ensuring policies and procedures are followed in regard to the standards set forth by the firm as they relate to graphic and production standards
- Working closely with outside consultants, such as specification writers, to articulate the firm's standards

STUDIO DIRECTOR: The studio director provides both managerial and operational support to the design team by implementing timelines, monitoring project activities, managing deadlines, and overseeing construction to ensure smooth delivery and completion of projects. The studio manager collaborates with principal and senior design staff to identify and define path and timelines for project scope, budget, and completion; ensure sufficient staffing; and identify and implement action plans to achieve firmwide goals and objectives.

> Primary responsibilities can include:

- Communicating with clients about project timelines, budgets, and overall project needs
- Generating and managing comprehensive project timelines and coordinating team workload assignments to ensure sufficient staffing on each project

- Managing timelines and implementation of projects with design teams (and as required, with general contractors, architects, and vendors) to stay on schedule
- Coordinating and implementing installation logistics in collaboration with head of purchasing, design teams, and assistant project manager
- Creating, administering, and tracking individual project budgets and collective budgets for all projects
- Hiring, supervising, and developing staff

OFFICE MANAGER: The office manager oversees the overall management of the office and office staff, from the supervision of administrative staff and interns to managing human resources, and manages all office meetings and events.

Specific responsibilities can include:
- Developing and overseeing all programs and procedures relevant to the administration of the office, including office organization and daily routines
- Managing recruitment and training, and scheduling timely reviews of employees
- Supporting and managing the functional areas of human resources, including maintaining personnel records, and compensation and benefits administration
- Implementing human relations policies/procedures and disseminating this information to all staff

CAD MANAGER: The CAD manager provides support to the design team to ensure proper use and systematic approach to the firm's drawing technology. A CAD manager also maintains copies of all drawings and maintains information regarding changes to the CAD database.

Specific responsibilities can include:
- Providing training and supervision of in-house CAD users and supplying technical support for all CAD software, including the

customization of CAD programs

- Providing production CAD support, including support for plotting and electronic file submissions, and producing corporate CAD screen shots
- Developing, implementing, and enforcing CAD standards
- Organizing the CAD environment, including maintaining CAD document archive and retrieval for projects, the cleanup of CAD files for project closeout, and archiving projects when completed
- Monitoring and maintaining CAD server, including daily backups

As important as it is to have a solid internal team structure, it's equally important to create one with your external resources. Depending on the type of project you're working on, you'll have to develop a team that may include any and all of these consultants: mechanical, electrical, plumbing, lighting, structural, acoustics, landscape, interiors, kitchen, storage, art. (In California you should include electric magnetic field and feng shui consultants.) The team also includes the contractor, the client representatives, the client, the project management team, and anyone having a decision-making role on the project.

The first thing to consider when forming the team is that each and every person is there to be an advocate for the client. As soon as one of the team members forgets that and tries to put someone in an adversarial position, the team starts to fall apart. Defining roles, clarifying responsibilities, and understanding who's accountable to whom will make this team a highly functioning structure.

When the teams are formed, the education of the client to understand the roles of each team member is vitally important. Clients often are concerned about each team member's roles and whether there'll be a duplication of effort. These are very natural concerns, and the answer is simple. There'll be some overlap, but if you trust your team, then they'll minimize the duplication and make the project and process run as efficiently as possible. The key word here is trust: when you trust your team and they prove trustworthy, the process is smooth.

Above all else, management reports that you share with your internal team should be shared with the external team as well. The more information that your entire team shares, the more connected and clear each team member will be with the project.

SCHEDULING

Scheduling your projects is one of the most important aspects of project management. It helps define the expectations of the client and the team, and assists with managing deliverables.

A project schedule creates a road map throughout the project. There should also be an officewide schedule that compares all projects and the phases they're in during a particular time period. These schedules can then be tied to fees, revenue projections, and backload.

A variety of good project scheduling software is available.* Most of our clients use Microsoft Project to manage their schedules. There are many others, however, that you can research to determine which one is the best fit for your firm.

BUDGETING

Budgeting for your projects is as important as scheduling. Any budget is only an educated guess, but it's essential for the successful management of a project. The budget you create for each project should address each phase the project will cycle through. In architecture those typical phases are predesign, schematic design, design development, construction documents, bidding, and construction administration. In interior design those phases may include preliminary concept development, design development and presentation, documentation, procurement, and installation. It's important to develop the budget to track not only time being spent on the project within each phase but also any anticipated expenses.

When establishing budgets for your projects, it's wiser to give your staff dollars to manage rather than just simply hours. The concern often raised is whether having access to the numbers

*For software recommendations, visit www.thebusinessof design.net.

on a project will reveal staff salaries. I personally don't think this is an issue, but if it concerns you, set your reporting to allow the numbers to be at billing rates rather than cost rates. This way you won't be sharing salary information. The bottom line is the more information you give people to manage their projects, the more successful you'll be as a firm in controlling those costs and maximizing the firm's profitability.

The easiest way to start budgeting for a project is to work backward. Most of the time you're given a finite schedule to run your project. The installation date or project completion date is a good data point to work backward from. Let's use the example of a project that'll be completed within eighteen months. If you have a fee of $450,000 to complete the project, this breaks down into $25,000 a month. Of course the time spent does not distribute evenly during the project, but as a baseline it's a good starting tool. You can then break the project into phases. Then you start building your team to understand who'll be on the project during these phases. You need to allocate the time expected of each person during each phase and divide the fees proportionally. This is just a starting point, because now you'll have to take your best guess and refine it to accommodate the fees by phase and staff. After just a few "tweaks," you'll have the workings of a meaningful budget.

Once the budget is established, you'll want to input the data into project-costing software that allows you to compare your budget by actual time spent. (SEE SAMPLE CHART, FIGURE 6) A good job-costing accounting system, which allows all time and expenses to be posted to specific projects, will be able to make the input and reporting of these data fairly simple. These tools are only as difficult to manage as you make them. Start out with the simplest approach, and if you require more detail, you can always add a layer of complexity. What I run into are firms that think they need to see every level of detail, and they then make the systems so complex that they don't really understand how to manage this information. The budget can be calculated using cost rates—although if I give people their cost rates, they can do the math and figure out what everybody in the

Office Earnings

Apple & Bartlett, PC

For the period 6/1/2010 - 6/30/2010

	Revenue	Total Billed	Unbilled	Received	A/R	Spent	Variance	Variance Percent
Project Number: 0001743.11 Children's Hospital Expansion								
Cur	27,122.13	27,122.13		27,122.13		27,122.13		
YTD	168,615.78	168,615.78		60,127.26	108,488.52	168,615.78		
JTD	168,615.78	168,615.78		60,127.26	108,488.52	168,615.78		
Project Number: 0020202.02 Martinville Children's Hospital								
Cur	14,111.67	14,111.67			14,111.67	14,111.67		
YTD	952,100.52	2,236,825.52	(1,284,725.00)	2,208,602.18	28,223.34	88,300.52	863,800.00	90.73
JTD	2,236,825.52	2,236,825.52		2,208,602.18	28,223.34	1,373,025.52	863,800.00	38.62
Project Number: 0021003.00 West End Women's Hospital								
Cur	23,982.01	23,982.01			23,982.01	23,982.02	(.01)	
YTD	725,745.06	1,705,320.06	(979,575.00)	1,657,356.04	47,964.02	149,900.12	575,844.94	79.35
JTD	1,705,320.06	1,705,320.06		1,657,356.04	47,964.02	1,129,475.12	575,844.94	33.77
Project Number: 0033090.90 VA Emergency Care Facility								
Cur	18,595.62	18,595.62			18,595.62	19,075.62	(480.00)	-2.58
YTD	116,586.22	116,586.22		79,394.98	37,191.24	119,466.22	(2,880.00)	-2.47
JTD	116,586.22	116,586.22		79,394.98	37,191.24	119,466.22	(2,880.00)	-2.47
Project Number: 0040101.01 Moscone School								
Cur	7,283.91	7,283.91			7,283.91	7,283.91		
YTD	44,468.46	44,468.46		37,184.55	7,283.91	44,468.46		
JTD	44,468.46	44,468.46		37,184.55	7,283.91	44,468.46		
Project Number: 0994628.92 Faulkner Clinic								
Cur	5,246.96	5,246.96			5,246.96	5,246.96		
YTD	152,431.76	152,431.76		40,443.92	111,987.84	33,921.76	118,510.00	77.75
JTD	356,431.76	356,431.76		220,443.92	135,987.84	151,171.76	205,260.00	57.59
Project Number: 1995097.00 North River Environment Test Laboratory								
Cur	15,521.99	15,521.99		31,043.98	(15,521.99)	15,521.99		
YTD	98,756.94	98,756.94		67,712.96	31,043.98	98,756.94		
JTD	98,756.94	98,756.94		67,712.96	31,043.98	98,756.94		
Project Number: 1999001.00 City Park Crosswalk Feasibility Study								
Cur								
YTD	(246.50)		(246.50)	54,002.00	(54,002.00)		(246.50)	100.00
JTD	138,040.00	113,716.50	24,323.50	113,716.50		139,021.00	(981.00)	-.71
Project Number: 1999004.00 GNH Music Center								
Cur								
YTD				24,721.63	(24,721.63)			
JTD	40,090.62	40,090.62		35,940.01		42,611.01	(2,520.39)	-6.29

FIGURE 6

Office earnings report from Deltek Vision software, an important report that summarizes a project's financial performance in three lines

FIGURE 7

Project progress report from Deltek Vision software, which analyzes a specific project's financial performance

158

Project Progress

Apple & Bartlett, PC   For the period 6/1/2010 - 6/30/2010

	Current Hours	Current Billing	JTD Hours	JTD Billing	Budget Hours	Budget Billing	% Exp	% Rpt	Balance Hours	Balance Billing
Project Number: 2003005.00 Adelphi Research Lab										
Phase Number: 1PD PreDesign										
Task Number: COD Code Analysis										
Labor										
00 General										
0 General			160	17,392	200	10,000	174	30	40	(7,392)
1 Principal	22	3,080	345	48,230	100	11,000	438	30	-245	(37,230)
Total for General	22	3,080	505	65,622	300	21,000	312	30	-205	(44,622)
04 Research										
P Planner					50	2,500		30	50	2,500
05 Scope Determin.										
1 Principal					60	3,000		30	60	3,000
09 Project Budget										
M Project Manager					25	1,250		30	25	1,250
10 Project Schedule										
M Project Manager					25	1,250		30	25	1,250
Total for Labor	22	3,080	505	65,622	460	29,000	226	30	-45	(36,622)
Expenses										
Reimbursable Expenses										
512.00 Mechanical Consultant						6,000		30		6,000
521.01 Meals		799		14,387						
522.00 Reproductions		230		7,015		5,500	128	30		(1,515)
524.00 Long Distance Telephone		384		6,914						
525.00 Postage/Shipping/Delivery		127		2,277						
527.00 Mileage		311		5,589						
529.00 Misc Reimbursable Expens		1,523		27,421						
Total for Reimbursable Expenses		3,373		63,602		11,500	553	30		(52,102)
Total for Expenses		3,373		63,602		11,500	553	30		(52,102)
Total for COD	22	6,453	505	129,224	460	40,500	319	30	-45	(88,724)
Task Number: PRO Programming										
Labor										
00 General										
0 General			219	18,983	300	15,000	127	30	81	(3,983)
Total for General			219	18,983	300	15,000	127	30	81	(3,983)
21 Proj. Admin.										
6 Administration					30	1,500		30	30	1,500
34 Field Survey										
E Engineer					30	1,350		30	30	1,350
44 Obtaining Permit										
6 Administration					15	675		30	15	675
Total for Labor			219	18,983	375	18,525	102	30	156	(458)
Expenses										
Reimbursable Expenses										
512.00 Mechanical Consultant						15,000		30		15,000
521.00 Travel,Meals & Lodging				8,970		20,000	45	30		11,030
521.01 Meals		518		9,315						
522.00 Reproductions		230		6,153		4,000	154	30		(2,153)
524.00 Long Distance Telephone		224		4,037						

159

GENERATED REPORT	TOTAL PRICE	PURCHASE COST	PROFIT
FILTERED BY INVOICE			
Sales Code: Fabric (1 record)	$518.40	$384.00	$134.40
Sales Code: Furniture (6 records)	$8,424.00	$6,240.00	$2,184.00
Sales Code: Time Billing (1 record)	$345.00	$0.00	$345.00
GRAND TOTALS (8 RECORDS)	$9,287.40	$6,624.00	$2,663.40

GENERATED CHART	SUM OF PROFIT
SALES CODE PROFIT: **LARGE, MEDIUM, SMALL**	
Sales Code: Fabric	$125.00
Sales Code: Furniture	$2,175.00
Sales Code: Time Billing	$350.00

FIGURE 8
Project profitability report
from Studio I.T. software,
which analyzes the
profitability of a specific
project by its different
income sources

office is earning. Alternatively, you can show your budgets at billing rates. Many employees have equal billing rates but unequal salary rates. This way they can still manage the dollars being expended at billing rates against your fees and be successful at this task.

To help validate the budget you'll want to compare your budget with other similar projects to determine if you're in range with what you've spent on previous projects. If these data aren't available, you'll need to use your best educated guess to determine if this is achievable. The good news is that as you accumulate more and more data, this process becomes easier. FIGURES 6-8

Let's start with the general philosophy of budgeting. If you have a budget of $1,000 and you give someone $1,000 to spend, they'll spend $1,000, if not more. However, if you give them $900, they may spend $900 and they may spend $1,000, but in both cases you'll be on or under budget. This plays into the 10 percent rule, which allows you to pull out 10 percent of your fees as a contingency and to manage with the 90 percent remaining. If you have skilled project managers and they can successfully manage the budget, your profits will be 10 percent higher. However, if unforeseen issues arise, this "surplus" is a contingency to cover those issues.

Creating the budget is only a small part of project management: the bigger piece comes from truly managing your resources in a successful way. An example of this might be how you manage your staff on projects by delegating certain tasks with specific hours associated with that task. This way they understand your expectations and perform accordingly. Another example may be managing consultants on your project by setting clear goals for them to accomplish their work within budget and on time. Once you have the reports to manage your resources, you actually have to learn what to do with these data. Having the information is only one part of the management process. Knowing how to use the information to manage the project should be your ultimate goal. If you notice that a project is beginning to exceed your budget, these reports can help you understand how to correct the project's course and bring the budget back on track.

Here's an example. You receive a report that shows during the previous month you've spend 20 percent more than you have in your budget. You also recognize that the project is limping along in a way that this pattern may continue for several months. If this continues, it won't be long before you'll eat up your entire budget and the project will be operating at a loss. You need to ask yourself the following questions:

1. Is the project simply going through a unique period and will it naturally correct itself, or is this a trend that'll ultimately kill the budget?
2. Will this situation continue and for how long?
3. What's at the heart of the problem? Do I have the wrong staff on the project? Are they being managed inefficiently?
4. Is this a client-driven problem? Should we be asking for additional services because this problem was caused by scope changes that are outside the initial services?
5. Is this simply a project in which we negotiated a fee that was too low to perform the work?

Whatever the answer is, the problem needs to be identified and addressed to be fixed. If it's a staffing issue, it may or may not be remediable, depending on your staff constraints. If it's a client issue, you'll need to communicate the situation to the client and propose a solution. If it's a management issue, then the project manager needs to jump in and fix it.

Budgeting the expense side of the project and managing the process involves an understanding of what real dollars you'll have to manage each project. These expenses are typically divided into reimbursable expenses and direct expenses. Reimbursable expenses are paid for by the client when they're incurred. Typically, firms charge a markup on these expenses for having to manage them and run them through the books. (For a more detailed explanation of this expense, see chapter 2.) Direct expenses are the costs directly related to the project and covered in your fees. These expenses can be consultant, travel, or printing costs. It's important to have your staff understand what the financial commitments are in the contract for this to be managed. If you allow these costs to get out of control, you can quickly eat up any profits. Experience is the ability to see a mistake before it happens *twice*.

CONTRACT MANAGEMENT

Similar to the financial data on a project, the more contract information you share—ideally, the complete contract—the better chance you'll have of your project being well managed. Having your contract available to your employees allows them to have access to and understanding of the scope of services and responsibilities the firm has committed to.

This may seem obvious, but first you need a contract. I can't tell you how many firms that have hired us to manage their office don't have a contract with their clients. The excuses are endless, but the potential results are disastrous. It doesn't matter whether it's a first-time client or one you've worked with for decades, or even your best friend, contracts exist for a reason. Like employee manuals, they help define your responsibility when things go bad. They should clearly spell out what's expected of you and what's expected of your client and what happens when either one of you doesn't perform.

Rather than outline every aspect of what the contract should cover—there are plenty of good books on this subject—I list some of the things we've added to our contracts because for one reason or another they're missing from the standard agreements we've been asked to negotiate.

1 Define an end date for the contract. Often projects get extended for reasons beyond your control, and it's important to put a realistic completion date in the contract.

2 Give as detailed a scope of services as possible. This helps define your commitment when the client is requesting additional work that should require additional fees.

3 Make it absolutely clear who your point of contact is on the project and who the ultimate client decision maker will be.

4 Make sure you have a "kill clause" in your contract. Most contracts include this, but it's one of the first clauses to be negotiated out. The importance of this clause is to protect the designer if the client puts the project on hold for an extended period of time. In all likelihood you'll have the capacity to commit to only a few projects per year, and if one of those projects stops, you'll have to replace that project with another. As you know from reading this book, the time to accomplish that could be as long as six months. The kill clause creates a penalty to the client that allows you to sustain your staff until you can replace the canceled project.

5 If you're an interior designer and you purchase antiques for your clients, you want language in your contract that protects you against verifying the authenticity of the antique. You should require your client to perform an independent appraisal of the goods and to make certain the liability is not residing with you, the designer.

6 It's very important when negotiating the ownership of documents that you protect your intellectual property and that clients understand that they're hiring you and your firm to provide a service and that any designs you create on their behalf are your intellectual property. If they want to own the designs, then you need to be compensated accordingly.

7 We've created a term called *Presented Price*. This is language used in interior design contracts to identify products that you'll be offering your clients at a price set by you and not a third-party vendor. The purpose of this language is to allow you to charge for the value of your designs rather than the cost of raw goods. If your contract provides for you to charge a markup on the cost of purchased goods, often it doesn't take into account the cost of goods that you custom-make for a client. If a client wants you to design a piece of furniture because there's nothing in the marketplace that's appealing and he or she likes your product designs, the cost of the labor and materials does not equal the value of your designs by simply marking up those raw costs with the typical markup. We instruct our clients to add a clause that allows for the designer to set a price that's equivalent to the value of the product created. This language compensates you for the perceived value of that good. In the end, of course, clients have the last say: if they think the custom product is too expensive, they can always pick something for sale in the marketplace.

8 We find that designers have a problem asking their clients to cover travel time to and from the job site or the client's location. This expense should be viewed as lost-opportunity costs. As long as you're working for a client, whether it's physically in the client's office, home, or site, or if you're traveling back and forth to those places, you're still working for that particular client. Our suggestion is that you determine a day rate for your time and that you charge clients that agreed-on day rate while traveling on their behalf. We've negotiated everything from charging 50 percent of our hourly rate while we're traveling to full billing rates. If you're traveling for more than one client, they should split those costs to be equitable.

9 Always have a clause that allows you to increase your billing rates annually. You'll typically increase your staff salaries every year, and if you don't adjust your rates, you're simply eating up your profit margins. If clients agree to this clause, the burden is on you as the designer to make certain you change your billing rates each year. I've worked with many firms that simply forget about this clause and wonder why three years later their billing rates are so low.

10 To protect your intellectual property, you should include language to make certain you're compensated if the project is repeated in another location. For example, if you design a restaurant and the client intends on creating multiple restaurants from one design, known as "rolling out," you should receive compensation for each rollout.

It's important if you agree to allow clients to roll out your designs that you also get them to indemnify you from any liability that may occur on the projects that you're not involved with.

An example of a major liability case occurred with a home designed to be built in the Southwest in a moderate climate. The owner took the drawings and built the house in the mountains where there was significant snowfall each winter. When the first snowfall came, the roof collapsed, because the structural engineers didn't anticipate the load factor for snow. The architect was sued and lost the case with the judge.

TECHNOLOGY AND PROJECT MANAGEMENT

No matter what I write on these pages, it'll change before the ink is dry. So here are a couple of helpful hints on dealing with the ever-changing environment of technology in design. Years ago, a designer could open up an office with an old door, two sawhorses, and a Mayline. Now the need for major capital investment in technology makes the opening of your practice a true financial commitment.

Where most firms get into trouble with keeping up on their technology is updating their hardware and software. The rule of thumb is that one-third of your equipment should be fairly new, one-third a year old, and one-third two years old. If you follow that formula, the annual investment is much less than if you let your computers all grow old at once and are forced to upgrade your entire office.

The other rule of thumb is that the faster equipment should be with the fastest people. If you have a whiz kid on CAD and he's stuck with a slow machine, or if you have a principal who barely uses the computer for anything other than text and spreadsheets and email, you're creating an inefficient scenario. In one case the person is being underutilized, and in the other the computer is being underutilized.

The other dilemma that many companies face is what software they need to purchase. This affects the hardware platform that you work off of. There are many consultants in the computer design world who can assist you in assessing your needs and determining what's right for you. What's most important in figuring out your hardware and software needs is to make certain that any consultant you use understands *your needs*. You may not have the type of firm that needs the fastest, most powerful hardware. Overcomplicating your needs can lead to a system that ultimately may fail for your company. We all tend to utilize technology to a fraction of its capabilities.*

POWER OF COMMUNICATION

The last point I'd like to make about project management is the power of communication. No tools, no budget, no software, and no schedule can ever replace the power of communicating well with your client. When you're open and honest about the issues, finding a solution is easier, and when you manage a client's expectations through good communication, the relationship thrives. The following story demonstrates poor communication and certainly poor customer service.

A client of mine called me one day to ask what he should do about a situation with the graphic design firm they recently hired. My client explained that he simply needed a reprint of some materials that they had already paid for. He thought this would be an easy task and was surprised to see a proposal come through for almost $1,000 for ten prints of a document that was completely designed and only needed to be printed and bound. He discussed the process and concluded that even though the price tag seemed high, the quality of the work was worth it, and the hassle-free communication of not having to pass this on to a third party would make it all worthwhile and quick to accomplish. He agreed to the $1,000 invoice and received the documents. Everyone was happy, because the product was in fact beautiful, and it truly showed that paying a little extra was worth it and the value was recognized.

Now fast-forward thirty days, to the arrival of the final invoice. It was $4,700. My client was shocked. The graphics firm knew how concerned he was about $1,000, so how could this have happened? After the shock subsided, the questions were asked. This was a reprint. How could you be so off on your quote if you've

For software recommendations, visit www.thebusinessof design.net.

167

Walker | Warner *Architects*

EXAMPLE RESIDENCE
Project Number: 2009-00

PRELIMINARY ESTIMATE OF DEVELOPMENT COSTS 8/26/09

ARCHITECTURE

	Area	Low	High		Low		High
Main Residence Conditioned Area	5,500 sf	$500	$700	$	2,750,000	$	3,850,000
Main House Garage & Covered Porches	500 sf	$350	$450	$	175,000	$	225,000
Pool House	600 sf	$450	$600	$	270,000	$	360,000

Estimated Building Construction Costs $ 3,195,000 $ 4,435,000

Use Avg. for WWA Contract Purposes $ 3,815,000

SITE DEVELOPMENT, LANDSCAPING, STRUCTURES AND ELEMENTS

				Low		High
Driveway	(+/- 9500 sq. ft.)	*allowance*	$	114,000	$	342,000
Entrance Improvements (gate, etc.)		*allowance*	$	25,000	$	40,000
Property Line Fence		*allowance*		T.B.D.		T.B.D.
Well Development		*allowance*		T.B.D.		T.B.D.
Site Utilities		*allowance*	$	25,000	$	50,000
Landscape Planting		*allowance*	$	50,000	$	200,000
Hardscape - Paving, Site Walls & Steps		*allowance*	$	150,000	$	300,000
Dock Improvements		*allowance*		T.B.D.		T.B.D.
Tennis Court		*allowance*	$	125,000	$	150,000
Generator		*allowance*	$	25,000	$	75,000

Estimated Site Development Costs $ 514,000 $ 1,157,000

	Low	High
Estimated Total Construction Cost	$ 3,709,000	$ 5,592,000

See next page for Professional Fees and Additional Costs:

NOTES TO ESTIMATE:
1
2

already done this entire process in the past? How could it ever cost $470 to print a soft-cover ten-page book? The anger came next. Why would you ever send a bill without explaining why the invoice would be almost five times the proposal? What gives you the right to spend $4,000 of anybody's money without permission?

The client told me it ended the sixteen-year relationship with the graphic design firm because instead of trying to reach out to my client and explain the situation to help him understand why the charges were so much more than expected, the graphic design firm responded with a simple email that said, "All charges are legitimate." This was an unfortunate way to end such a lengthy relationship, but the vendor didn't understand the value of communicating with a long-term client. We've all heard the expression "never burn bridges." Or as George Strait says in his song "By the Light of a Burning Bridge": "It's amazing what a man can see by the light of a burnin' bridge."

> "A person who never made a mistake never tried anything new." —*ALBERT EINSTEIN*

Richard Meier

Keith Granet: In my opinion, the Getty was a commission of a lifetime. Was it in any way a turning point for you?

Richard Meier: I don't know if it was a turning point. We had a lot of work in Europe; it may have been a turning point in terms of my work in the United States. Certainly it's the largest commission in my lifetime, here or abroad. In a sense, it's certainly the most important project in my career.

KG: If you were asked to identify the ideal client, who would that be?

RM: Generally, the most ideal client is an individual who may represent a group but who is involved and is as committed to the project as the architect. An individual who is there all the way through and wants to make something significant.

KG: Do you feel in Europe the respect for your role is significantly different?

RM: It's totally different. It's just a different attitude.

KG: How would you describe it?

RM: I'll describe it with one incident that is very memorable for me. We did a building in Paris for a private corporation, a television broadcasting company. It's a wonderful building, but it was on a very tight time schedule, because they had to move from their existing headquarters to the new office as well as the new studio space. During construction we realized that the glass we had for this fairly transparent building had this kind of bluish-greenish

cast to it, which was standard in France. We wanted to use a clear glass, so we approached the biggest French glass manufacturer. But it wasn't available through them. The only clear glass we could get was glass from Germany. We could get it in time, but it would cost more money. At that time, we were building a mockup of the facade panel on the site to show the president what the difference was. We went to Paris and had a meeting on the site. When he looked at the mockup, the president turned to me and asked, "Richard, you think that having a clear glass is important to the building?" I turned to him and I said, "Yes, I do." He said, "Well, then we'll do it." He valued my judgment, my aesthetic opinion; that's why he hired me. That's why he believed in me and what I was doing for him.

KG: The president of the French television station seemed to understand the distinction between building a structure just to house themselves and building a structure to be proud of.

RM: And they're very proud of it. I'll never forget that incident, because it was not his decision; it was my decision. He knew I was concerned about his spending money as much as if it were my own.

KG: Did you walk out of there thinking, "I can't believe he just asked me that question"?

RM: No, I could believe he could ask me the question, but what I couldn't believe was his immediate response. It wasn't, "I'll think about it" or "Let me talk it over with other people." It was, "I respect you and I'll do whatever you think is important."

KG: What would you tell students if they thought they only wanted to be an architect?

RM: I think you have to really want to do it. If you really want to do it, you should do it. But if you're thinking, "I'd like to be an architect, doctor, lawyer, or something else," then you should do something else.

KG: So you think it should really be in the blood.

RM: Yes, I think it has to be your passion. I think that's true of being good at any profession. It's what you really want to do. Because you can do a lot of things well, not just one thing, for the most part. You should do the one that gives you pleasure.

KG: A lot of people strive to achieve success, but there's only a handful of people who really make it.

RM: A lot is luck.

KG: Do you think that's how your name has gotten out there? I'm sure the quality of your design is a big element of your success.

RM: I think I've been lucky. Lucky to choose architecture as my profession. I was lucky to know what I wanted to do. I was lucky to have a good education and work in very good offices and to start my own firm when I was young. I began working in my apartment in one room, and living and sleeping in the other room. As time went on, I got a little bit more to do and couldn't take out the laundry in the middle of the day, so I decided I better get a real office. I was lucky to get commissions that enabled me to practice.

KG: I wonder about the first time you saw one of your buildings being built.

RM: The first time I saw one of my buildings built was a little house that I did on Fire Island. It was built in nine days. We slept on the site, the workers and myself. It was nothing but this little beach house. It was a great thrill. I think that's the same thrill that I've always felt and continue to feel when I see a work completed.

KG: Do you think you could ever see yourself retiring?

RM: No. I don't see any reason for retiring. What am I going to do?

KG: How would you like to be remembered as an architect?

RM: I think that the work I do is unique in many respects. The level of quality makes it distinctive and enduring in a way that will benefit society long after I'm gone. People will enjoy and use the fruits of our labors for a long, long time. It will give pleasure and uplift the spirit for people who have not even been born yet. That thought keeps me going and keeps me working to achieve something. It makes being here worthwhile.

CHAPTER 6

Product Development

Although product development is not meant for every design business, it's rapidly finding its way into many firms. Products branded with designers' names have quickly become the norm when introducing a new product line. For this reason, I felt compelled to add this chapter in a book about the business of design. Product development can have many advantages for your design business and can help expand your name recognition to a broader marketplace.

Product development has been the fastest-growing part of Granet and Associates in the past five years, and for many of our clients it's been the fastest-growing part of their businesses as well. One reason is the attention to good design from companies such as Design Within Reach, IKEA, Williams Sonoma, Restoration Hardware, Target, and many others, which have created a new level of appreciation for design by the general public. I'm often asked if there's actually any more room to add designers' names to products, considering the flurry we've been experiencing. My answer is always the same, yes. When you walk into a department store and see the walls littered with fashion designers' names, it doesn't faze you, because you're used to it. Even though designer brands in the home-furnishing world are common, the number of names getting attention from the consumer today is significantly higher.

I began my entrée into the product-development sector fifteen years ago with the launch of the Barbara Barry Collection for Baker Furniture. It was wildly successful and taught me that I enjoyed working with both designers and manufacturers to collaborate on new collections. Today we have forty-five lines in the marketplace and approximately the same number in negotiations. Our phone rings daily with designers and manufacturers interested in developing new lines.

The first thing we tell potential clients is that just because you've designed products for your individual clients doesn't necessarily mean that you can design products for the masses. To be truly financially successful in product design, you need to design for the masses, and if not the masses, then you need to have a very special product offering that has great appeal to a wide audience in our profession. Designing a beautiful chair for one client does not make a product line.

I wish I could tell you that it's all about skill, talent, and design, but it's about so much more, and some of the factors seem rather nebulous as well. Sometimes it's just about being in the right place at the right time. What I do tell potential clients is that the most successful designs are ones that fill a need in the marketplace. Something that you always look for but you can simply never find. When you fill those voids, the product is usually a hit.

Another important factor that I tell clients when we first start working with them is that you must keep your design practice running. Even if you're wildly successful at product development, it's important to keep designing for your clients. You can scale this portion of the practice way down once you've developed a robust product program, but you should still have private clients. The reason for this is that your design firm is your sandbox. It's the place where new ideas are conceived and tested, and there's no better place to do this than your design firm. When you're only designing products, you tend to lose a connection to the end user, and your design firm allows for that connection.

Let me share with you a story about a client, Suzanne Kasler, who wanted to break into product development. She approached us because she already knew exactly what the product line should look like. She was located in the Southeast and had minimum exposure in the national shelter magazines. We met in New York to discuss her goals and designs, and immediately I liked her. We began our search to try to sell her ideas. Right after she signed the contract, she mentioned that the only furniture company she wanted to design for was Hickory Chair. This was our first challenge, since Thomas O'Brien, Alexa Hampton, and Mariette Himes-Gomez—all high-profile New York designers—were already on its roster.

I headed to the High Point furniture market and set up a meeting with Jay Reardon, president of Hickory Chair. Jay reviewed the brand book presentation but wanted to run it by Thomas O'Brien to first see what he thought. Thomas had noticed the attention Suzanne had received during the previous months in shelter magazines like *Elle Décor*, *Traditional Home*, and *House Beautiful*. We met, and the deal was made over the next couple of weeks.

I tell you this story because it was one part about Suzanne's designs, one part about the right fit for her and Hickory Chair, one part about the press she was receiving at that particular moment, and one part about who she was as a person. None of these parts could stand alone, but together the alignment created the perfect timing and perfect recipe. This was just three years ago, and today she is on her way to building a major brand with six licenses and a few more in the works, and a new book.

HIRING A LICENSING AGENT

I do believe that you should have a person representing you to build your licensing program. We once had a potential client who decided he would try it himself first, and if that didn't work out, he'd call us. At one of the home furnishings markets we ran into him, and his first response was, "This feels like I'm trolling for partners." It is trolling: trying to sell yourself is difficult, and people tend to respect it only if you have someone representing you on your behalf. It's also important to separate the design talent from the business negotiations. It's a little bit like playing good cop/bad cop. As a designer you want to focus your energy on the designs and not on all the details of closing and managing deals. Even so, plenty of people have successfully started their own brands without hiring a licensing agent. It all depends on what you're capable of handling and how you want to approach this endeavor.

What you should expect from having a licensing agent is someone who's well connected within the industry to make the proper introductions but also someone who has the inside story on which companies are looking to expand their licensing offerings. A licensing agent needs to be in constant touch with what's happening in the marketplace as well as have direct correspondence with the industry's decision makers. Otherwise, the agent's just knocking on doors to see which ones open. You want someone who attends all the international and national trade shows, and there are many of them.

You also should expect that your agent can handle your deal from *A* to *Z*. The process begins with an understanding of your brand and its position in the marketplace and then moves to identifying potential partners, negotiating agreements with the right partners, managing agreements until the product launches, and finally managing the relationship from a marketing, financial, and operational approach. It's appropriate to think of your agent as a partner in the success of your program, who has as much a vested interest in your success as you do.

Compensation for agents is all over the board, but you should expect to pay a percentage of your royalties that they obtain for you as part of their compensation. Some agents also charge a monthly retainer while they're searching for deals.

This investment requires a significant financial commitment. You should not get into the field unless you have the financial wherewithal and time to do it properly. This is a financial investment in your future, and it may be a minimum of two years before you see any return on the initial investment. If that's not possible, it's best not to pursue product development. It seems like a long time to wait, but when you think about the many phases, it's not long at all.

Building a brand and a product line is illustrated in our Product DNA graphic. FIGURE 1

PRODUCT-DEVELOPMENT PROCESS

The first step is a brainstorming session to gain a strong under-standing of the brand as well as a strong understanding of the goals of the designer or manufacturer, depending on who's hiring us. This session explores the categories that the designer is passionate about as well as deep exploration into who he or she is and what the brand may look like.

We try to gain as much knowledge as possible about the audience that a particular designer wants to reach. If your audience is large because you have television exposure, we might look for retail partnerships. If your audience is the design profession that knows your work through trade publications, we may align the designer with a trade showroom. We're diligent about making certain that we don't try to take a designer to a mass audience before there is mass awareness. If we had an unlimited marketing

PRODUCT-DEVELOPMENT DNA

The following diagram walks you through the process of bringing a product line to market and the responsibilites of each of the participants in the process.

Graphic used to articulate to Granet clients the product-development cycle

1 STAGE 1: Product Conception

Enter into Granet/Designer Product development Agreement

GRANET & ASSOCIATES
MARKET RESEARCH | 4 WKS

- Ⓐ Marketplace
- Ⓑ Financial Capacity
- Ⓒ Demographics
- Ⓓ Price Points
- Ⓔ Potential Manufacturers
- Ⓕ Potential Retailers

DESIGNER
Product Development | 4-8 WKS

- Ⓐ Schematics and Drawings
- Ⓑ Renderings
- Ⓒ Colors Palette
- Ⓓ Materials
- Ⓔ Finishes

LEGAL | PATENT RESEARCH
8 WKS

- Ⓐ TM Research
- Ⓑ Confidentiality

2 STAGE 2: Product Development

Enter into Granet/Designer Product development Agreement

GRANET & ASSOCIATES
DESIGN + PACKAGING | 4 WKS

- Ⓐ Evaluate and Critique Design
- Ⓑ Packaging Development
- Ⓒ Continued Research on Manufacturers and Retailers
- Ⓓ Contract Negotiations

DESIGNER
Product Development | 4-8 WKS

- Ⓐ Dimensioning
- Ⓑ Refining Materials
- Ⓒ Refining Finishes
- Ⓓ Design Refinement
- Ⓔ Renderings
- Ⓕ Models (3D/Physical)

3 STAGE 3: Prototype

GRANET & ASSOCIATES
PROTOTYPE REFINEMENT | 4 WKS

- Ⓐ Critique Design
- Ⓑ Fine-tune Prototype Changes

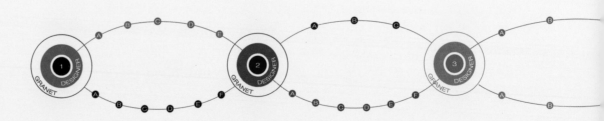

4 STAGE 4: Marketing   **5** STAGE 5: Manufacturing & Distribution   **6** STAGE 6: Product Management

GRANET & ASSOCIATES
MARKETING | 4 WKS

A Identification
B Name/Logo Design
C Packaging Design

GRANET & ASSOCIATES
MANUFACTURING | 8-24 WKS

A Contract Negotiations
B Fabrication
C Retailer Distribution/Buyers

GRANET & ASSOCIATES
MARKETING | ONGOING

A Tradeshows
B Tear Sheet
C Website
D Press
E Launch

LEGAL | PATENT RESEARCH
8 WKS

A Copyright
B TM/Patent

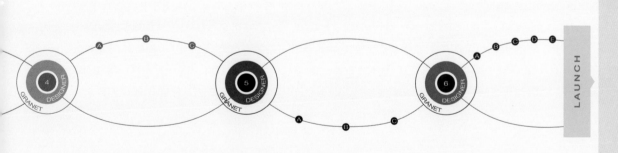

budget, we'd be more lenient about this rule. But rarely if ever are we presented with unlimited marketing budgets. We may discover that a designer has great mass appeal, but currently his or her work is recognizable only by the design trade. We build the brand through fabrics and furniture in trade showrooms, and once that program is up and running we look for partners who have a more consumer-based audience. This allows us to build brand awareness first in categories such as bed and bath and tabletop, and then to move to bigger categories such as furniture and lighting to a mass audience because the designer is beginning to build brand loyalty by the consumer.

If you think about whom the average consumer knows in the home furnishings brand arena from a named designer, it would be only Ralph and Martha. I don't need to name their last names because their brands are that strong. Interestingly enough, neither one of them comes from the home design world. Ralph comes from fashion, and Martha from entertaining and publishing. The top recognizable people in our industry who have built brands that consumers might know are people such as Thomas O'Brien and Barbara Barry. Jonathan Adler has done a good job with his brand, but he also comes from a different profession. Fashion icons have come into the home category for years, Calvin Klein, Bill Blass, Oscar de la Renta, Donna Karan, Fendi, and Armani, because they have huge brand loyalty and trust that will follow them almost anywhere. So why is it that interior designers have had a hard time becoming recognized in the public eye? Marketing is one reason; interest in the category is another. Home furnishings are not impulse buys and do not get replaced as frequently as fashion lines, so there's less consumer recognition for brands.

But the tides are turning in the right direction, with more and more interest in home design television programming that has invested significant airtime in our industry. Mostly these shows are devoted to the makeover, but more programming is being added regularly that addresses all aspects of the design profession. Names like Thom Filicia and Nate Berkus were born from television, but both of them also started out with successful design firms. The brands that we're building today will be the household names of the future. The internet and the exposure of these brands will become more and more commonplace, and it'll become, not unlike fashion, acceptable to associate a designer's name with home furnishings.

We caution potential clients to make certain they start their licensing programs at the highest point of entry in terms of price point. As their brand becomes better known, they can start moving down the marketplace to the masses. If you start high, you can always go down, but if you start low, it's much more difficult, some say impossible, to go up.

THE BRAND BOOK PRESENTATION

Once we've completed a strategic plan for our clients, we then move that plan into action with a beautiful brand book that articulates the essence of the designer. The books we create with our clients always have two parts. The first part is an aesthetic peek into the designer's creativity, and the second is a press portfolio. The success of the line is truly about the product, but what sets the collection apart is the designer and what he or she brings to the marketing and promotion aspect for the companies he or she aligns him- or herself with. Companies are very interested in how much the press follows a designer. The designer's ability to attract editorial coverage for the collection allows manufacturers to gain exposure that doesn't require tremendous amounts of advertising dollars. The combination of editorial and advertising coverage makes the connection to a designer brand very appealing. If a designer is a media darling, then the chances of getting great exposure for the collection in the press are improved.

The brand book is a tool that can quickly reveal what a company can expect to get from a designer. It's often made the difference between simply hearing a name and the ability to demonstrate the designer's value that can seal the deal. Here are some examples of very successful brand books. FIGURES 2-4

FIGURE 2
Brand book for Campion
Platt

FIGURE 3
Brand book for Suzanne
Tucker Home

FIGURE 4
Brand book for Mary
McDonald

RESEARCHING POSSIBLE COLLABORATORS

Once the brand book is ready, the next steps are to present it to manufacturers that you've identified in your strategic plan. This may come in the form of a one-on-one meeting with manufacturers or at trade shows, such as High Point, Maison Objet, Neocon, the New York Gift Show, or the tabletop show.* The most successful meetings come when you've made contact with the company's decision maker. The brand book should give the decision maker a sense of the design and the designer to gauge his or her compatibility.

In the research phase we often start by asking a designer to list his or her favorite resources. This usually helps us understand the caliber and aesthetic of the manufacturers we should approach. It's also helpful when you're presenting a designer to a manufacturer and that designer is a good customer of that manufacturer. The designer knows the brand, and usually the aesthetic, and connection comes much quicker. Sometimes the opposite can happen, and a manufacturer doesn't understand why a particular designer is a good fit. On one occasion, we had a client who wanted to design Tibetan rugs, but the manufacturer wasn't sure about working with the designer because the rugs were all made of sisal. It turned out that the designer always used sisal because there weren't simple beautiful rugs in the marketplace, and the designer had great ideas to fill that void. This successful collection has been available for over ten years now.

Sometimes the collaboration seems to be a stretch for both the designer and the manufacturer, but there may be a quality about the work that connects the two. We have put unlikely partners together because their business visions were similar and the quality of product was similar, but they had never stretched themselves in a certain aesthetic direction. All the best business deals come from entrepreneurial people who can think beyond their current offerings.

On another occasion I walked into a showroom and asked to speak with the president about licensing, and the response was that the manufacturer didn't license designer's collections. I asked if there might be some interest in exploring the possibilities. His response was

*For a list of the most popular shows, visit www.thebusinessof design.net.

surprising. He said the company had thought about it but didn't know how it worked, and asked if we would be interested in explaining the process. From that point forward, we knew we were educating the manufacturer on the process and had to explain it in a way that was simple yet appealing. This was a textile collection for Charlotte Moss at the kickoff meeting. She and I walked into the manufacturer's conference room, and hanging there on the product development board was a bed Charlotte had designed in her own home. It turned out that it had been there for months, and the company was using it for inspiration. The synergy was already in place before we even started designing the line. The best deals come together when there's some other force in play that connects the team.

The truly innovative companies take advantage of economic downturns to start looking for collaborations to create a buzz when the market turns around. If a business is holding back in hard times, then when the market turns it'll have very little new product to show and probably won't be able to catch up in time to weather the upswing. When the economy is slow, there are still buyers with needs, just fewer of them. Having new products in a downturn keeps you fresh and helps the consumer know you'll be around even in the worst of times. This also helps build brand loyalty. Interestingly enough, when we see 30 percent fewer people at trade shows, it doesn't correspond to a 30 percent drop in sales. This is because the people who continue to come to trade shows are the serious buyers. When the market falls, the casual shoppers are the ones who fall off, and the pool of buyers becomes much more serious.

BUILDING A BRAND HIERARCHY

Although there are no hard-and-fast rules to building a brand, it's easier when the development builds in this direction: furniture, lighting, rugs, textiles, decorative accessories, wall art, bed and bath, tabletop. (There are other categories such as outdoor, hardware, broadloom, and office, but they're often supplemental to the brand you've first established.) The reason this hierarchy is successful is that each product tends to support the next product. If you first have furniture, then the furniture retailers tend to want to round out the collections with the other categories. If you start with lighting or textiles, you may not need furniture to promote the initial products, and the exposure for the brand can be limited.

The first license is the hardest one to obtain. This is because the first license is taking the biggest risk in working with a new designer. Once a designer has that first license, it then gives great comfort to other potential manufacturers, knowing that the risk is being shared.

Another aspect of the licensing is the difference between licensing your name and licensing your designs. Once you have a recognizable brand you may be asked to license your name. This simply means that you're attaching your name to products that you have little or no design control over. This is where we tend to see celebrities and fashion designers enter the home market. Because their names are so recognizable, many companies are willing to slap a label on their products and pay the person a royalty for the use of his or her name. At the end of the day, it's the quality and design of the actual product that sells, not the label. FIGURE 5

NEGOTIATING THE DEAL

Once you've established which manufacturers to collaborate with, you need to negotiate the terms under which you'll work. We always start with what we call a term sheet. This document calls out the key deal points in the agreement, such as royalty rate, product naming, marketing requirements, number of designs, launch date, length of the deal, and any special requests. If the manufacturer agrees on these initial terms, we then move to the contract. The following are specific points that we include in every contract.

1 **TERM:** We typically limit the term of our agreements to three to five years. They're always renewable. If the term isn't specified, the contract needs to give you the right to terminate. If either party is not performing up to expectations, you need to have the ability to move in a new direction.

LICENSING TERM SHEET

DESIGNER:	Joe Smith
MANUFACTURER:	ABC Home Furnishings
PRODUCTS:	Textiles Collection
MARKS:	Joe Smith for ABC Home Furnishings
TERRITORY:	US and Canada plus ABC Website and Catalog
TERM:	3 years
REPORTING:	quarterly, within 30 days afer completion of each quarter. (1/1:3/31=4/30; 4/1:6/31 = 7/30;7/1:9/31 = 10/30;10/1:12/31 = 1/30)
EXECUTION FEE:	Upon execution of the agreement a $20,000 advance will be given to the Designer
RENEWAL:	3 years if mutually agreed upon
PROVISIONS:	If a design does not make it into the marketplace within 12 months to launch, design rights revert back to designer. All products will be marked as Joe Smith for ABC Home Furnishings
ADVERTISING:	$100,000 in advertising costs in year of launch and 2% of sales in all subsequent years. Advertising and packaging to be developed by Manufacturer in direct collaboration with and final approval by Designer. Production, materials, and media to be managed by manufacturer with input and approval from Designer.
DESIGN:	All Designs will be executed from Designer's office. Submitted materials will nclude: concept boards, color palettes, reference images, digital files. Designer shall be reimbursed for all incurred expenses to assist in prototyping.
ROYALTY:	6% of net sales, paid quarterly along with Royalty Report, within 30 days after completion of each quarter. Net sales are gross sales with deductions for returns and samples.

GUARANTEED
MINIMUM ROYALTY:

Year 1:	$20,000
Year 2:	$30,000
Year 3:	$40,000

CHANNELS OF
DISTRIBUTION:

All products will be distributed in retail stores, website and catalog. Samples: 1 (ONE) Production sample of every item will be supplied to Designer at no cost. Additional samples will be invoiced at wholesale.

APPROVALS:	Designer must respond with comments or approvals within 10 business days of Manufacturer's submission, or submissions are deemed approved. This provision applies to: product, packaging, and advertising collaterals.
EXPENSES:	Travel expenses will be reasonably reimbursed if they have been discussed and if budget has been previously approved by Manufacturer.
AGREEMENT TO AGREE:	The parties agree to negotiate in good faith a formal license agreement upon the terms hereof, containing the standard terms and conditions customary in such license agreements, to be executed within 30 days from the date of this term sheet.

2 MILESTONES FOR PERFORMANCE: If a collection consistently sells at an increasing rate, it'll be renewed. But if the collection ever drops less than 20 percent from the average of the last three years of sales, the designer has the right to terminate the agreement.

3 LABELING: Specify how the products will be labeled and branded. (For example, Suzanne Tucker's furniture license with Michael Taylor Designs indicated that the collection be labeled "The Suzanne Tucker Home Collection for Michael Taylor Designs.") It's important that there's consistency in the brand both graphically and textually. This builds brand recognition, which will be useful for any collaborations associated with the brand.

4 ROYALTY RATES: These rates vary by product categories. On average the royalty rate is 3 percent on the low end and 12 percent on the high end. This will vary based on volume and name awareness of the brand. If the licensor is too demanding with the royalty rate, then the collection's price point will need to increase, and that can make or break a collection.

5 DESIGN CONTROL: Do not relinquish design control to the manufacturer. Always retain the rights to approve and sign off on all designs and quality control.

6 MARKETING: On average allocate a minimum of 2 percent of sales to marketing the product. In the first year of launch, designate a minimum amount of dollars to promoting the launch. This will vary depending on manufacturer and category.

7 ADVERTISING: If the manufacturer has an advertising program, we request that 50 percent of all advertising pages be devoted to the new product during its first year of launch. In all subsequent years we request that the line receive equal coverage between all lines carried by that manufacturer, that is, if there are four licensed lines with a manufacturer, then each product line should receive one-fourth of the advertising pages.

8 SAMPLING: The designer should receive one free sample of each product he or she designs, and should also have the right to buy additional products at wholesale cost for personal use. This is good for the manufacturer, because it helps promote the products.

FIGURE 5 A typical term sheet used by Granet and Associates to present the business terms of a licensing deal

9 LIABILITY: Place all of the product liability on the manufacturer. This is the benefit of a licensing agreement. The designer is taking a small percentage of the sales for the use of his or her designs, but in exchange doesn't have to take on the risk associated with manufacturing and distributing the products.

10 TERRITORY: Grant the right to sell in territories where the manufacturer has distribution. If the manufacturer doesn't have distribution, then we want to leave those territories open to others who can distribute of behalf of the designer.

11 EXCLUSIVITY: Only grant an exclusive license for a category if the manufacturer is able to commit to a large volume of sales. Otherwise, it's okay to grant exclusive rights to the designs but not to the entire category.

12 LAUNCH DATE: Call out a launch date. If the products do not come to market within this time frame, the designs will revert back to the designer, who's free to bring them to another manufacturer.

13 ADVANCES: An advance against royalties can be negotiated to help defray the designer's costs in developing the line. The manufacturer might argue against offering advances, due to the significant costs associated with prototyping and launching the line, and the designer should be responsible for some of the start-up expenses. Our success in receiving the advance depends on the manufacturer's desire to obtain the license. The stronger the desire, the higher the advance.

14 MINIMUM GUARANTEES: This requires the manufacturer to actively market the products to meet the minimum sales in a specified time period.

15 EXPENSES: We require a manufacturer to cover all expenses associated with designing the line, including all travel expenses to visit the manufacturer during the prototyping phases and to market and promote the line at any point of distribution.

As I've already mentioned, any deal must be beneficial to all parties in order for it to be successful. All of these deal points are fair and reasonable. The success of the collaboration is based on the teamwork created between all parties. As soon as the deal is good for only one of the parties, it will collapse.

MANAGING THE DEAL

Once the deal is signed, then the fun begins. Designing the product requires a schedule and a detailed matrix of responsibilities for each party. The clearer you are about responsibilities, the easier the process will be to meet the launch target. FIGURE 6

Once the product has launched, the relationship will require ongoing management. The best relationships have longevity. For this to occur, there needs to be someone managing the process to allow for it to be kept moving and improving. Some of the steps required in good management of a product line are as follows:

1 Management and review of quarterly reports and royalty collections

2 Semi-annual review of product successes; if a product is not selling, it needs to be determined why and whether it's a fixable problem or if the product should be removed from the collection

3 Augmenting the collection; annual reviews to determine new products to add to the collection

4 Annual review of other possible categories associated with the manufacturer to expand the collection

LICENSING VERSUS SELF-PRODUCTION

A common question for designers is whether they should license their designs or produce the designs themselves. Licensing is the more common avenue in product design simply because of the start-up costs associated with self-production. The profits are considerably higher in self-production, but so are the risks. The main reason to self-produce any line comes from a desire to control the outcome, control the quality, and control the distribution, and with that comes all the risk and expense. To determine whether you should license or self-produce, ask yourself the following questions.

FIGURE 7

PRODUCT-DEVELOPMENT SCHEDULE

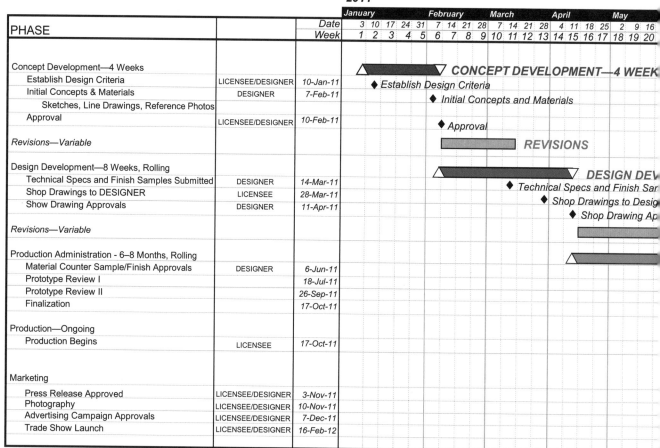

PHASE		Date	2011
		Week	January — May timeline

PHASE		Date
Concept Development—4 Weeks		
Establish Design Criteria	LICENSEE/DESIGNER	10-Jan-11
Initial Concepts & Materials	DESIGNER	7-Feb-11
Sketches, Line Drawings, Reference Photos		
Approval	LICENSEE/DESIGNER	10-Feb-11
Revisions—Variable		
Design Development—8 Weeks, Rolling		
Technical Specs and Finish Samples Submitted	DESIGNER	14-Mar-11
Shop Drawings to DESIGNER	LICENSEE	28-Mar-11
Show Drawing Approvals	DESIGNER	11-Apr-11
Revisions—Variable		
Production Administration - 6–8 Months, Rolling		
Material Counter Sample/Finish Approvals	DESIGNER	6-Jun-11
Prototype Review I		18-Jul-11
Prototype Review II		26-Sep-11
Finalization		17-Oct-11
Production—Ongoing		
Production Begins	LICENSEE	17-Oct-11
Marketing		
Press Release Approved	LICENSEE/DESIGNER	3-Nov-11
Photography	LICENSEE/DESIGNER	10-Nov-11
Advertising Campaign Approvals	LICENSEE/DESIGNER	7-Dec-11
Trade Show Launch	LICENSEE/DESIGNER	16-Feb-12

Timeline labels from chart: CONCEPT DEVELOPMENT—4 WEEK; Establish Design Criteria; Initial Concepts and Materials; Approval; REVISIONS; DESIGN DEV; Technical Specs and Finish Sam; Shop Drawings to Desig; Shop Drawing Ap

FIGURE 6
Product-development
schedule depicts the
timeframe from conception
to launch of a new product
line.

2012

July	August	September	October	November	December	January	February	March
20 27	4 11 18 25	1 8 15 22 29	5 12 19 26	3 10 17 24 31	3 10 17 24 31	7 14 21 28	2 9 16 23 30	6 13 20 27	5 12 19 26
25 26	27 28 29 30	31 32 33 34 35	36 37 38 39	40 41 42 43 44	45 46 47 48 49	50 51 52 53	54 55 56 57 58	59 60 61 62	63 64 65 66

NT—8 WEEKS
tted

REVISIONS

PRODUCTION ADMINISTRATION - 6-8 months

terial and Finish Sample Approvals
♦ Prototype Review I

♦ Prototype Review II
♦ Finalization

PRODUCTION

MARKETING
♦ Press Release Approved
♦ Photography
♦ First Advertising Approvals
♦ LAUNCH

1. Is manufacturing your core competency?
2. Do you have the ability to distribute the products to achieve significant sales?
3. Do you have the capital required to produce the products?

FIGURE 7 Fortuny textiles

If the answer is yes to these three questions, producing your own products is a viable alternative.

Here's a case study to help you understand what's involved. We had a client who wanted to produce a fabric line. She had a great love for textiles and knew how to produce and design textiles. What she lacked were the resources to make the textiles (or a connection to the mills) and the ability to distribute them. But a few of her favorite multiline showrooms indicated interest in representing them if they created a line. She began by visiting local printing houses to see what was necessary to create a printed collection. It became quite evident that a printed collection, although the least expensive route to launch, was not going to satisfy her desire for a meaningful collection, because her work was known for beautiful textiles that included wovens and velvets and jacquards, not just prints. The next step was to visit Proposte, the invitation-only textile show in Lake Como, Italy. Mills present their offerings, and a designer or a textile distributor has the choice of buying a particular fabric or leasing it with limited distribution. In addition, you can bring your designs to the represented mills and have them create original designs on your behalf. For a textile lover, this show is Disneyland.

Once relationships are formed with the different mills, the designing begins. Some designs are inspired by historical documents collected through the years, and others are original designs. Once the products are in production, all the other tasks and costs become evident. First, each design and colorway requires a minimum order to be committed to. This can be one of the biggest expenses. Additionally, there are the expenses associated with selling the line, including production pieces for displays and memo samples, logo creation, hang tags, business cards, sales kits, and photography.

The investment is substantial, but the hope is that instead of receiving a 5 percent royalty as in a licensing agreement, there will be a 40 to 50 percent margin on sales. The final step before production can begin is to approve the strike-offs in the case of fabrics or prototypes in the case of furniture, lighting, or other home products.

The next step is to determine where to sell these products. In this case the right place was high-end trade designer showrooms. We then identified the right showrooms for the collection and set up meetings with each showroom to introduce the collection. The collection was well received, and the product was launched in five cities: San Francisco, Los Angeles, New York, Chicago, and Paris. We will eventually address other major markets once the collection has had a chance to gain exposure in these first five cities.

When self-producing a line, the burden of inventory and distribution lies with the designer. You must be prepared to handle these tasks and all the costs associated with this new company. We typically don't recommend self-producing unless you're prepared to make the product line a new business and a core competency within your current business. Another option for designers who have distribution through their own retail store or an online e-commerce website is to have companies produce private label products for them. A private label means that a manufacturer will produce the goods under the designer's label at a cost significantly lower than market. These products are packaged exclusively for the designer. This eliminates the need for designers to manufacture the goods themselves. The profits in this scenario are better than licensing, but this method also requires designers to have their own distribution outlets.

BUILDING YOUR BRAND

In building a brand that will create consumer recognition and brand loyalty, you must be deliberate about how your brand is presented in the marketplace. Simple things are not always obvious. FIGURES 8–11

The following are our rules of thumb in building a brand.

1 It starts with a great name. It can be your name, but first make certain your name makes sense in connection to your brand and the business you're building.

2 If your goal is to build your brand and eventually sell it, then be careful about using your name, because you'll have to sell it for its brand equity in the future. For example, Rachel Ashwell sold her name along with Shabby Chic and had to buy her name back when the investors in Shabby Chic went bankrupt.

3 A strong logo is necessary.

4 Consistency in the graphic presentation is best. We had a client who was building her brand, but every time you saw her picture it looked different. She placed her picture with every product she made, and in every ad the picture was different. This was not a good approach, because the visual connection you make to a brand happens in a nanosecond, and if you confuse your audience with different visuals, they'll never connect to your brand.

5 It is recommended whenever possible not to align your face with your brand.

6 Create a point of view that's easily grasped.

7 Don't surprise your audience unless you're introducing a new collection, and even the new collection should make sense to your followers.

8 Describe the brand in one sentence or even one word, the shorter the better.

9 Position yourself in the right marketplace, and remember to start high and then go down, because you can never reverse the trend. FIGURES 13–15

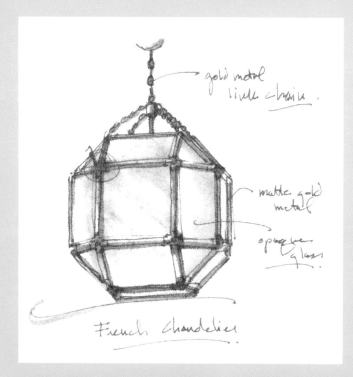

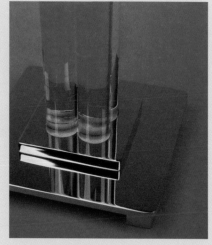

FIGURE 8
Drawings of Morris light
fixture in development

FIGURE 9
Finished Morris light fixture
for Visual Comfort

FIGURE 10
Lamp developed by Thad
Hayes for Boyd Lighting

FIGURE 11
Detail of Thad Hayes lamp

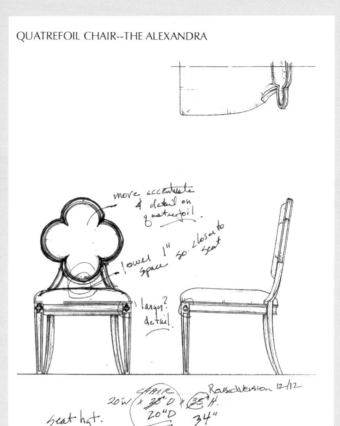

QUATREFOIL CHAIR--THE ALEXANDRA

FIGURE 12
Van Cleef and Arpels
inspiration for the Alexandra
Chair

FIGURE 13
Drawings of the Alexandra
Chair

FIGURE 14
Drawing of Thom Filicia's
Century Club chair for
Vanguard Figure

FIGURE 15
The Century Club chair

CONCERNS OVER BEING KNOCKED OFF

Very often designers are concerned about having their designs knocked off when we present them to manufacturers to determine if there's interest in collaborating. In most cases we present the manufacturers with a nondisclosure agreement, and in most cases they're happy to sign this agreement. However, when you build a solid brand you *will* be knocked off. The true defense for the brand is not chasing all the knockoffs but in building a brand that has loyalty and a strong following. You want to build a brand that people prefer. Who actually wants to be the one competing with Apple for the iPad or iTouch? Plenty of companies will build more powerful versions and less expensive versions, and that'll attract enough people to buy enough of them to make some profit, but it'll never take away meaningful market share because of the brand equity of Apple. If you build a solid brand, the brand itself will carry as much weight with your consumer as the actual product.

Although imitation is inevitable, especially with increased success, I don't recommend you stand by and let someone continue to knock off your designs. We've sent around our fair amount of cease-and-desist letters. But you can spend all your time with attorneys if you let it distract you and not focus on your business.

MASS MEDIA AND YOUR BRAND

It's easier to spread the word when you develop your brand if you're involved in any sort of mass media: television, web presence, movies, or major print campaigns. When we first signed the interior designer Thom Filicia as a client, it became clear that his power had just as much to do with his television exposure as his design talent. Mass media exposure offers you the ability to reach a mass audience and ultimately mass sales.

The power of mass media is ever changing. QVC (quality, value, and convenience) and Home Shopping Network (HSN) have been around for almost three decades and have proven that home furnishings can be purchased through these channels. The internet has certainly made a significant mark on consumer purchasing

FIGURE 16 Samples of products (left to right): Anouska Hempel's line of cosmetics for Zelens; Tucker & Marks candle; Rose Tarlows candle.

FIGURE 17 Suzanne Tucker Home Fabric Collection

FIGURE 18 Charlotte Moss for Pickard China

of furnishings for the home and office. There are significant web portals that have captured market share through their sites. These sites are popping up regularly and will continue to grow as long as consumers have confidence that they can make successful major purchases from the internet. As the traditional landscape of retail changes and distribution shifts from mainly bricks and mortar, it's important to be aware of how to represent your brand in each channel as clearly and concisely as possible. FIGURES 16–18

> "I don't design clothes, I design dreams." *—RALPH LAUREN*

199

CONCLUSION

The intention in writing this book was never to educate its audience about every facet of the design business. My goal was to provide a solid understanding of running a successful design practice and what elements need to be considered. I wanted to share stories from my career that helped me learn this business and help others navigate their way. I wanted this book to be visually exciting, to inspire the creative mind with illustrations in a way that can often tell a story better than with words alone. If the small amount of wisdom that I've offered here improves the design profession even slightly, then this book will have done its job.

The knowledge I obtained over the years did not come without mistakes, practice, stretching my limits, and pushing myself to see things in different ways. We live in a world that changes so rapidly, I suspect there will be plenty of new material in another five years.

For now, I hope you, the reader, will walk away with information that allows you to think about your career, your profession, and your firm in a new and healthy way. Like building or designing a home tailored for a client, each one of you will take away a different view of this book. My hope is that the information I provided will help you build the firm that is right for you. Take the advice I suggest here in any way that works for you, and use it in a way that allows you to keep your voice, your style, and your practice as a true reflection of you.

Thank you for allowing me the privilege of sharing my thoughts with you.

ACKNOWLEDGMENTS

Building a career around helping design professionals think of their work as a business is not an easy mission, but one that I have embraced and enjoyed for almost thirty years. Along the path of building my career there have been many people who have mentored, influenced, and guided me. I would like to acknowledge these people as well as everyone involved in making this book into a reality.

On a very personal level, I honor my grandmother Anna Davis, who taught me how to value my work. To all my family and friends who have supported me not only during the writing of this book but also while I was building my career.

My career would not be what it is today without the support and friendship of my clients. Each one of them has given me purpose in my work, and they are individually acknowledged on pages 204–5.

I extend my deepest appreciation to the many people who worked closely with me on this book. They include David Beach, Stan Charnin, Jennifer Kirshman, Melanie Robinson, and the "once an English teacher always an English teacher" Jim Vaszauskas. Karyn Millet for her beautiful photography. Without a doubt this book would never have happened without the amazing support and magical guidance of the unflappable Christine Tope.

The work of Granet and Associates is the result of a collaborative effort from our talented team. I would like to acknowledge, Alison Jones, Andrea Panico, Jon Vaszauskas, Christopher Taylor, and Zak Graff.

At Princeton Architectural Press, I would like to thank Kevin Lippert, Jennifer Thompson, Linda Lee, and Deb Wood for their support and guidance, which has allowed the creation of this beautiful book.

This book is here only because of the support and amazing efforts of Jill Cohen—there is no one more skilled at her job. I will thank her every day for helping me realize this opportunity, but mostly for the friendship that has come out of this endeavor.

I want to acknowledge Art Gensler for his willingness to write the foreword and for the mentorship he gave me early in my career. I was blessed to have him show me the way.

I thank Beth Farb for her sage advice and coaching, which helps me improve every day.

A very special acknowledgment goes out to Cindy Allen and Pilar Viladas for the support they have shown me; and to my "Design Leadership Summit" partners, Meg Touborg and Peter Sallick; together we have built a community of design professionals that feeds my soul.

I get to wake up each and every day and do what I love because of so many people who support my life: Monique Gibson, Marianne Nelson, Suzanne Tucker, and Keith Recker—I treasure your guidance, support, and love.

CLIENT LIST

Abe
Addis English & Associates
Algert Engineering
Altoon + Porter Architects
Amanda Nisbet
Amelia T. Handegan, Inc.
Anita Brooks Interiors
Anouska Hempel Design
Anshen + Allen
Appleton & Associates
Arquitectonica
Babey Moulton Jue & Booth (BAMO)
Banks Design Associates, Ltd
Barbara Barry, Inc.
Barbara Lee Grigsby Design Associates
Barry Design Associates
Beckson Design Associates
Bilhuber & Associates
Brockmeier Consulting Engineers, Inc.
Brown Jordan
C R Studio
Calvin Klein
Campion Platt
Carde-Ten Architects
Carolyne Roehm
Celerie Kemble Interiors
Charlotte Moss Inc.
Chris Barrett Design
Cisco Brothers
Clodagh

Concept Studios
Chris Mestdagh
Danielian Associates
David Hertz Architects, Inc.
Deborah Nevins Associates
Diamond & Baratta
Doc Williamson
Donghia
Douglas Durkin Design
Douglas Whitmore & Associates
Drake Design Associates
Dujardin Design
Eleish Van Breems
Ellis-Clark Design Group
Ergo
Felderman Keatinge & Associates
Ferguson & Shamamian Architects
Finton Construction
Fortuny
Frederick Fisher & Partners Architects
Fremer\Savel
Gafcon, Inc.
Gensler
George Smith
Gerald Allen Architects P.C.
Giannetti Architecture & Interiors
Gilt Groupe
GP Schafer & Associates

Grace Home
Gruen Associates
Gunkelman-Flesher
Hardy Holzman Pfeiffer Associates
Harrods, Ltd.
Hayakawa Associates
HCA Partners
Hirsch Bedner Associates
HOK
Hollyhock
HOM Escape in Style
Hornberger Worstell Architect
Huntsman Associates
IBI/ Blurock Group
I. Grace Company
Ike Kligerman Barkley Architects
Ilan Dei
Interior Architects, Inc.
Island Architects
J Oakley Associates
James Radin
Janus et Cie
Jed Johnson Associates
JAM Design, Inc.
Jiun Ho
Johannes Van Tilburg & Partners
John Barman Designs
John Varvatos
Johnson, Wen, Mulder
Jonathan Adler
KAA Design
Kaplan Gehring McCarroll

Karastan
Kathryn Ireland
Kelly Harmon Interiors &
  Decoration
Kenneth Brown
Killefer Flammang
  Architects
Kittrell Garlock &
  Associates
Koning-Eizenberg
Kostow Greenwood
Kramer Design Group
Landry Design Group
Landworth Debolske
  Associates
Lee, Burkhart, Liu, Inc
Linda London, Ltd
Lindmark Engineering
Loews Inc.
Lori Weitzner Limited
M Arch
Magni Design
Marmol Radziner and
  Associates
Mary McDonald, Inc.
Mia Lehrer
Monique Gibson
Moule Polyzoides
Nadel, Inc.
Naomi Langer Studio
Nate Berkus Associates
Nathan Egan
ND+SM Design
Neumann Mendro
  Andrulaitis
Nickey Kehoe
NotNeutral
ODA Design Associates
Opuzen
Ove Arup & Partners
Pacific Environmental
  Group

Pamela Burton &
  Company
Pantone
Paul Alan Magil & Assoc.,
  Inc.
PBS&J
PCR
Penco Engineering
Perlman Architects, Inc
Peter Block
Peter Schifando
Project Solutions, LLC
RMC Architects
Richard Meier and
  Partners
Richard Mishaan
Richard Sol Architect, Inc.
Rios Clemente Hale, Inc.
RipBang Studios
Rob Sinclair
Rob Wellington Quigley,
  FAIA
Rose Tarlow Melrose
  House
Sean O'Connor Lighting
Sebastian Construction
SFA Design
SF Jones Architects
SGPA Architecture and
  Planning
Shawn Henderson
Shimahara Illustration
Soicher Marin
Starr Design Group
Steve Chase Associates
Steven Ehrlich Architects
Stewart\Romberger &
  Associates
Suisman Urban Design
Suzanne Kasler Interiors
Suzanne Lovell, Inc.
Suzanne Rheinstein
Suzanne Tucker Home

Tara Shaw Designs, Ltd.
Technicon Computer
  Services
Texeira Design
Thad Hayes, Inc.
Thom Stringer Design
  Partners
The Neiman Group
Thom Filicia, Inc.
Thomas Callaway
  Associates
Tichenor-Thorp Architects
Tim Barber, Ltd.
  Architecture & Interior
  Design
Tim Clarke, Inc.
Trend Union
Trittipo and Associates
Tucker & Marks
TY INC
Victoria Hagan Interiors
Walker Warner Architects
Wallace Cunningham, Inc.
Waterworks
Wells & Fox Architectural
  Interiors
Wheeler & Wheeler
Whisler Patri Architects
Widom Wein Cohen
William Hefner Architect,
  Inc.
William Hezmalhalch
  Architects, Inc.
Withee Malcolm
  Partnership

INDEX

ABA Journal, 99
accountability, 64
accountants, 30, 61, 75, 95, 106
accounting
    billing and, 73
    job-costing, 157
    project budgets and, 66
    software packages for, 58–60, 59
    two methods of, 46–47
accounts payable/receivable, 35, 47
    balance sheets and, 48
    frequency of data review, 61
    in purchasing reports, 56, 57
    reports on, 50–51
accrual method, of accounting, 46–47
Adler, Jonathan, 180
advances, against royalties, 188
advertising, 181, 187
aesthetics, 59, 93, 107
    design directors and, 153
    niche marketing and, 96
airline in-flight magazines, 99
Alexa Hampton Furniture Collection, 175
Alexandria Chair, 196
American Institute of Architects (AIA), 20, 41, 90, 94, 107, 123
American Society of Interior Designers, 94
Appleton & Associates website, 89
architects
    accounting software for, 58
    celebrity status of, 13
    client relationships with, 79
    education of, 21–24
    "pay when paid" terms and, 51
    pricing practices, 20
    project architect, 149–50
    registered, 129
    reputation of, 20
    with small incomes, 14
    startup of design firms and, 31
architecture
    billing methods for, 67–68, 69, 70–72
    changes in practices, 78–79
    commercial, 70, 71
    as commodity, 41
    hierarchy in firms, 23
    institutional, 70
    job titles and roles, 148–50, 152–55
    as luxury, 106–7
    project phases in, 156
    residential, 70, 71
    as responsibility, 106
Armani, 180
Ashwell, Rachel, 195
assets, list of, 48
award submissions, 104
awareness, creation of, 91–93

backlog, 86
Baker Furniture, 174
balance sheets, 48
bank balances, 35
banking firms, 95
Barbara Barry Collection, 174
Barry, Barbara, 180
Bauhaus, 79

bed and bath, 184
Berkus, Nate, 180–81
bidding, 68, 156
Bill Blass, 180
billing, 16, 161
    contracts and, 165
    cost per square foot, 71–72
    cycle of, 69–70
    hourly, 67, 70–71, 165
    lump sum, 71
    percentage of construction, 67–68, 69, 70
    for reimbursable expenses, 73–74
    by value rather than hour, 13
    See also fees/fee structures
blogs, 99, 103, 103–4
bonuses, 64, 75, 125
bookkeepers, 13, 30, 35, 44, 50
book publication, 104–5
Boyd Lighting, 195
brands/branding, 13, 187
    brand books, 181, 182
    brand loyalty, 180, 184
    building of, 194, 195–96, 197, 198, 199
    hierarchy, 184–85
budgeting, 34, 61, 97, 106
    annual operating budgets, 61–62, 63, 64–65
    frequency of data review, 61
    profit planning reports, 47–48
    project budgets, 65–66
    project management and, 144, 156–57, 158–60, 161–63, 168
    See also expenses
building audits, 21
building information modeling (BIM), 68
business cards, 84, 86, 90, 91, 192
business plans, 24, 25, 26–28, 29, 33
business practices, top ten, 35, 36–37, 38–39

CAD (computer-aided design), 128, 138, 154–55, 166
Calvin Klein, 180
Campion Platt brand book, 182
cash flow, 13, 51, 70
cash journal, 50
cash method, of accounting, 46–47
celebrities, 185
Century Club chair, 196
Chanel, Coco, 105
Chanel fashion house, 24
charities, 89
checking account statements, 35
chief executive officers (CEOs), 128
chief financial officers (CFOs), 23, 44, 128
chutzpah, 16, 91
clients, 45, 78
    billing and, 67–68, 70–73
    communicating with, 91–92, 167, 169
    ideal/perfect, 41, 79, 95, 107, 138, 170
    looking for, 38
    management of, 13
    patron clients, 92
    product development and, 174–75

project management and, 141, 155
    public relations and, 98, 101, 104
    relationships with, 111, 113
    staff and, 109
    turning down jobs from, 97–98
    value appreciated by, 46
codes, building, 150
common sense, 16
communication, 38, 167
    listening skills, 110–11
    postproject, 91–92
    project management and, 167, 169
community, 90, 106
    creation of, 93, 93–96
    social media and, 102
competitions, 28, 40–41
computers, 64, 166
construction administration, 65, 68, 156
construction costs, 45, 65, 67–68, 69, 70
construction documents, 149, 151, 156
consultants, 81, 95, 141
contractors, 95, 149, 155
contracts, 51, 66–67
    contract management, 163–66
    term negotiations, 185–89
core values, 25, 27–28
credit cards, 48, 50
credit lines, 30, 48, 56, 57
culture/skill chart, 113, 114, 115
custom-designed products, 73, 164–65
customers, 28

data, review of, 60–61
debt, 48
delegation of tasks, 17, 122, 126
    Direct/Coach/Support/Delegate chart, 118, 119, 120
    job captains and, 149
deliveries, 150
Deltek Vision software, 46, 49, 58
    budgeting reports in, 158–59
    fee-invoice sample, 69
Departures magazine, 99
design
    business aspects of, 20
    control of, 187
    as craft, 19
    design development, 65, 68, 69, 156
    design education, 21–24
    as luxury profession, 20
design assistants, 151–52
design consultants, 31
design directors, 127, 152–53
designers
    celebrity status of, 13, 20
    collaboration with manufacturers, 183–84
    project budgets and, 65
    reputation of, 20
    responsibilities of, 151
    with small incomes, 15
    superstar, 14
design firms
    economic recession and, 32–33
    employee benefits, 124–25
    legacy firms, 132–33

ownership transition in, 130
partnering with outside
    resources, 29
startup of, 30–33
structure of, 126–29
vision statements of, 26–27
Design Leadership Summit, 94
Design Within Reach, 174
Direct/Coach/Support/Delegate
    chart, 118, 119, 120
discipline, 16, 38
Disney, Walt, 137
distribution, 188, 189, 192, 193, 199
Donna Karan, 180
draftspersons, 52, 128, 147, 150
Dunham, Arthur, 132

e-commerce, 193
education allowances, 125
Einstein, Albert, 169
Eisner, Michael, 98
Elle Décor magazine, 175
Elrod house, 136
Emery Roth, 41
employee benefits, 28
employee handbooks, 66
employee practices insurance, 74
employees. See staff (employees)
end users, 95
engineers, 50, 128
equipment, 30, 48, 75, 166
equity, 48
errors-and-omissions (E&O)
    insurance, 73–74
Excel software, 55
exclusivity, 188
executive summaries, 55–56, 57, 61
expeditors, 128, 152
expenses, 13, 61, 66
    accounting systems and, 46, 47
    cash journal and, 50
    clients' approval and, 68
    direct, 162
    executive summaries and, 36,
        56, 57
    general ledger and, 48
    insurance, 64
    negotiation of deals and, 188
    ownership transition and, 131
    photography, 105, 192
    project management and, 156
    project-related reports and, 52
    reimbursable, 64, 73–74, 162
    of self-production, 192
    10 percent rule and, 76
    travel, 65, 165, 186, 188
    See also accounting; budgeting

Facebook, 103
fashion industry, 180, 185
feasibility reports, 21
fees/fee structures, 16, 45, 67, 76
    See also billing
Feldman, Simone, 139
Fendi, 180
Ferguson & Shamamian Architects
    website, 89
Field of Dreams phenomenon, 61
Filicia, Thom, 180–81, 196, 197
financial statements, 35, 36–37,
    61
financial tools, 46–47
firing, 16, 61
fixed expenses, 64
Fortuny textiles, 192
401(k) plans, 125
furniture/furnishings, 175, 180, 193
    brand hierarchy and, 184, 185
    brand recognition, 180, 181
    markup on purchase of, 72–73,
        164–65
    mass media and, 197, 199
    purchase of, 152
    selection of, 151
Gehry, Frank, 96
general contractors, 31
general ledgers, 48, 50

Gensler (Gensler and Associates/
    Architects), 14, 110
    internships at, 123
    marketing in culture of, 82,
        86–87
    vision statement of, 24
Gensler, M. Arthur, Jr., 75, 86–87, 124
goals, 28, 33
Granet and Associates, 13, 34, 45
    accounting software used by, 58
    annual operating budgets of, 64
    interview process at, 115–16
    product development, 174
    public relations with clients, 101
graphic designers, 30
Graves, Michael, 40–41, 98
Gropius, Walter, 40
Guggenheim Museum Bilbao, 96

Hagan, Victoria, 95, 138–39
Hayes, Thad, 93
health insurance, 74, 124
Helmuth Obata and Kassabaum
    (HOK), 132
Hempel, Anouska, 198
Hickory Chair, 175
High Point, 175, 183
Hines, Gerald, 98
hiring, 13, 16
    culture/skill chart and, 113
    "hire/fire firms," 61
    interview process, 115–16
    practices, 126
    studio directors and, 154
holidays, paid, 54, 62, 125
Home Shopping Network (HSN), 197
hotels/hospitality, 70
House Beautiful magazine, 175
human resources, 16, 110–11
    culture/skill chart, 113, 114, 115
    listening skills, 111, 112, 113
    office managers and, 154
    principals and, 148

IKEA, 174
income (profit-and-loss) statements,
    47
installation, 65, 151, 152, 154, 156
insurance, 31, 64, 74–75, 95
intellectual property rights, 164, 165
interior design
    bachelor's degree in, 21
    billing methods for, 72–73
    hierarchy in firms, 23
    job titles and roles, 150–55
    licensing not required for, 21
    project phases in, 156
interior designers, 31, 58
International Style, 79
Intern Development Program (IDP),
    of AIA, 123
internet, 181, 197, 199
interns/internships, 14, 123, 128, 139
    in design firm hierarchy, 23
    responsibilities of, 150
    time analysis reports and, 52
inventory, 193
investment firms, 95
investments, 48, 166
invoices, 50, 167, 169
    See also billing
iPhone applications, 103
IT support, 31

Jefferson, Thomas, 39
job captains, 23, 127
    project budgets and, 65
    responsibilities of, 149
    studio structure and, 147
    time analysis reports and, 52
job descriptions, 127
job signs, 93
John Saladino Group, 24
Johnson, Jay, 132
Johnson, Jed, 132
Johnson, Philip, 40, 79, 98

KAA Design, 24
Kahn, Louis, 107
Kasler, Suzanne, 175–76
key man insurance, 74
"kill clause," in contracts, 164
knockoffs, 197
knowledge, 16, 21
Kohn, A. Eugene, 106–7
Kohn Pedersen Fox Associates, 26,
    106–7

labeling, 187
Lake|Flato, 24
landscape designers, 33
launch dates, 185, 188
Lauren, Ralph, 180, 199
Lautner, John, 136
lawyers/attorneys, 31, 94, 99, 106
    knockoff designs and, 197
    ownership transition and, 131
Lecours, David, 101
legacy firms, 132–33
liabilities, 48, 164, 165–66
liability insurance, 74
libraries, sample and resource, 150
licensing, 13, 14, 129
    of architects, 21–22
    brand hierarchy and, 185
    collaboration with manufacturers
        and, 183–84
    exclusive, 188
    licensing agents, 176–77
    self-production versus, 189,
        192–93
    term sheets, 186
lighting, 151, 155, 180, 193
    brand hierarchy and, 184, 185
    product development and, 195
listening skills, 111, 112, 113
loans, 48
logos, 29, 34, 192, 194
lump sum billing, 71

magazines, 99, 100, 175
mailings, regular and holiday, 101, 102
Maison Objet, 183
management, 21, 28
    business/financial, 43
    cash-flow problems and, 51
    firm structure and, 126–27
    retreats for, 133
management consultants, 31
manufacturers, 95, 183–84
    knocked-off designs and, 197
    negotiation of deals with, 185–89
Mariette Himes-Gomez Furniture
    Collection, 175
marketing, 13, 16, 81
    awareness, creation of, 91–93
    building a plan for, 87, 89
    as discretionary expense, 64
    market size and locations, 28
    negotiation of deals and, 187
    niches, 96–97
    principals and, 148
    product development and, 177,
        180
    public outreach, 88–91
    public relations and, 82, 100
    in startup of design firms, 30–31
    timelines, 82, 83–85, 86–87
marketplace, high and low positions
    in, 181, 194
Mary McDonald brand book, 182
mass media, 197, 199
meal expenses, 65
Meier, Richard, 170–71
mentoring, 17, 122–24, 139, 151
    Direct/Coach/Support/Delegate
        chart, 118, 119, 120
    tennis ball exercise and, 121, 122
Merrill, John, 78
Michael Graves and Associates, 40
Michael Taylor Design, 187
Microsoft Project, 156
mission statements, 16, 26
Morris light fixtures, 195

Moss, Charlotte, 184, 198
Myspace, 103

name recognition, 173
names, licensing of, 185
Nelson, George, 40
Neocon, 183
networking, 91
newspapers, 99–100
New York Gift Show, 183
niche markets, 96–97, 123

O'Brien, Thomas, 180
office managers, 128, 154
office space/structure, 28, 30, 32
office supplies, 64
One Minute Manager, The, 118
operational budget reports, 47
ordinances, city, 150
Oscar de la Renta, 180
ownership transition, 129–32

paid time off (PTO), 125
partners
    in architecture/design firm
        hierarchy, 23
    choosing, 128–29
    licensing agents and, 176–77
    ownership transition and, 130–31
    project titles and, 127
    retirement of, 78
passion, importance of, 14, 16
"pay when paid" terms, 51
Pedersen, Bill, 107
performance milestones, 187
philanthropy, 89
photographers, 100
Pickard China, 198
portfolios, 34
predesign, 156
principals/partners-in-charge, 23, 124,
    127, 150
    project budgets and, 65, 66
    responsibilities of, 148
    retreats and, 134–35
    review of project reports, 60
    staff reviews and, 117
    time analysis reports and, 52
printing expenses, 65
private labels, 193
problem solving, 138
product design, 20
product development, 17, 138–39, 173,
    174–76
    brainstorming, 177, 180–81
    brand book presentation, 181, 182
    brand building, 194, 195–96, 197,
        198, 199
    collaboration with
        manufacturers, 183–84
    licensing agents and, 176–77
    management of deals, 189
    negotiation of deals, 185, 186,
        187–89
    Product DNA graphic, 177,
        178–79
    schedule for, 189, 190–91
production directors, 153
products, 28, 109
    custom-designed, 73, 164–65
    end users of, 95
    naming of, 185
    private label, 193
    samples of, 198
    social media and, 103
    vendors and, 31
profitability, 75, 160
profit planning reports, 47–48, 49
profit sharing, 64, 75, 125
project budgets, 65–66
project management, 17, 28, 141
    budgeting, 156–57, 158–60,
        161–63, 168
    communication and, 167, 169
    contract management, 163–66
    decision making, 144
    expectations, 144

scheduling, 144, 145, 156
team for, 144, 146, 146–47,
    148–56
technology and, 166–67
vision statements, 142, 143–44
project managers, 127
    budgeting and, 161, 162
    in design firm hierarchy, 23
    project budgets and, 65
    responsibilities of, 148–49
    review of project reports, 60
    time analysis reports and, 52
project-related reports, 51–52, 53, 54
project-to-date figures, 51
promissory notes, 132
promotions, 38
Proposte textile show, 192
public relations (public outreach), 16,
    81, 88–91, 98–100
    agents, 31, 100, 102
    award submissions, 104
    book publishing, 104–5
    holiday mailings, 101, 102
    marketing and, 82
    social media and, 102–4, 103
punch lists, 149
purchase orders, 54, 59–60
purchasing reports, 54–56, 55, 57, 61

QuickBooks software, 58
QVC channel, 197

Rand, Ayn, 77
real estate
    agents/developers, 31
    leases, 74
    profession of, 20
Reardon, Jay, 175
references, checking of, 116
referrals, 81, 84
relationships, building, 111
rent, 64
repeat business, 92
Restoration Hardware, 174
résumés, review of, 116
retreats, company, 122, 133, 133–37
"reverse ego," 96
reviews
    of deals with manufacturers, 189
    of staff, 38, 110–11, 116–18, 154
Richard Meier and Partners
    Architects, 27, 170–71
Rios Clementi Hale Studios website,
    89
risk-taking, 16
Robb Report, 99
Rockefeller, David, 106
Rogers, Rutherford D., 104
rollouts, compensation for, 165
Rose Tarlow candles, 198
Rottet Studio, 27
royalty rates, 185, 187, 193
Rudolph, Paul, 107

salaries, 64, 161
sampling, 187
savings, 76
scale models, 150
scheduling, 156
schematic design, 65, 68, 69, 83, 156
self-production, 189, 192–93
senior designers, 127, 150–51
Shabby Chic, 194
shares, sale of, 131, 132
sick time, 54, 62, 125
signature look, 96
Skidmore, Owings & Merrill (SOM),
    78, 132
social media, 99, 102–4
software, 46, 55, 58–60, 59, 157,
    166–67
speaking, public, 88, 104–5
staff (employees), 17, 82
    annual operating budgets and,
        61–62, 63
    benefits for, 124–25
    communication and, 38, 39

culture/skill chart and, 113, 114,
    115
in hierarchy of architecture/
    interior design firms, 23
job titles and roles, 146, 146–47,
    148–56
mentoring of, 118, 119, 120, 121,
    122–24
as primary asset, 109
relationships with, 111
retreats and, 134, 137
reviews of, 38, 110–11, 116–18, 154
support for, 61
10 percent rule and, 76
start-up costs, 188, 189
starving-artist syndrome, 15
stationery, 34
Stern, Robert, 98
stock, sale of, 131, 132
Strait, George, 169
strategies, 28, 33–34
Studio Designer software, 46
studio directors, 128, 153–54
Studio I.T. software, 58, 160
studio system, 146, 146–47
suppliers, 95
Suzanne Tucker Home
    brand book, 182
    Fabric Collection, 198

tabletop show, 183
tactics, 28
talent, 16, 45, 81, 95
Target, 174
taxes, 47, 73, 75, 76, 106
teams, project, 144
    job titles and roles, 148–56
    studio structure, 146, 146–47
technology, 28, 31, 107, 138, 153,
    166–67
television, 20, 177, 180, 197
10 percent financial rule, 35, 38, 76
tennis ball exercise, 121, 122
term sheets, 185, 186
territories, right to sell in, 188
textiles, 139, 192
    brand hierarchy and, 184, 185
    selection of, 151
Thad Hayes lamps, 195
Thomas O'Brien Furniture Collection,
    175
time cards, 60
timelines, project, 153–54
time-off benefits, 125
titles, promotional, 128
Town and Country magazine, 99
trade shows, 176, 179, 180, 183, 184
Traditional Home magazine, 175
transmittals, 149
travel expenses, 65, 165, 186, 188
"treadmill theory," 135
trust, 68, 71, 89, 155
Tucker, Suzanne, 187
Tucker & Marks candles, 198
Twitter, 103

vacation time, 54, 62, 125
value, 46, 67, 167, 181
Van Cleef and Arpels, 196
Vanguard Figure, 196
vendors, 31, 81, 95, 164
Victoria Hagan Interiors, 89, 138–39
vision statements, 16, 24, 26–27, 142,
    143–44
Visual Comfort, 195
Vogue magazine, 99

wall art, 184
Walt Disney Concert Hall, 96
websites, 89, 92–93, 93, 103, 193
Welch, Jack, 76
Williams Sonoma, 174
workers' compensation, 75
Wurster, Bill, 79

Zelens, 198